CW00798619

Anne's commitment to supporting postgraduate r
this comprehensive guide.

Gill Houston, Chair,
UK Council for Graduate Education

A must-read to tackle research projects effectively … an exceptionally practical
resource for research students.

Dr Anna Gannon, University of Cambridge

This book is essential reading for postgraduate students who want to gain
as much as possible from their work and complete their research on time.

Professor Dag Husebø,
University of Stavanger, Norway

If you are an early stage researcher seeking reassurance and guidance on
undertaking a research project, you must read this book. It takes you stage by
stage through the process of designing and carrying out a research project,
helps with common problems, team work, lack of motivation and problem
solving. It also assists you in dealing with feedback and managing your time
effectively. The book should be on every emerging researcher's desk.

Professor Rosemary Deem, Royal Holloway,
University of London

An essential guide for doctoral students as they navigate the way to becoming
tomorrow's research leaders.

Professor Alistair McCulloch,
University of Southern Australia

Successful Research Projects

Comprehensive and accessible, *Successful Research Projects* provides a practical, research-based framework to help examine practice, solve problems and plan research effectively. With key practical tips throughout, it draws on examples from across disciplines and across the world ensuring best practice for those completing projects in the fields of science, health care, social sciences, arts and humanities as well as multi-disciplinary projects.

This book covers the key questions, challenges and solutions, exploring:

- organising time effectively
- working effectively with colleagues
- getting the best out of a supervisor and understanding what help is available
- demonstrating good practice in academic writing
- differences between research projects at undergraduate and postgraduate levels
- staying motivated and balanced in order to excel throughout the process
- looking at ways to use research to help career planning.

Providing the significant theories behind ways of managing projects, identifying important goals and solving problems, *Successful Research Projects* is the perfect companion for the busy student facing a postgraduate research project.

This is the companion guide to the second edition of *Successful Research Supervision*, a research-based practical framework for academics to examine and develop their effectiveness as supervisors. It helps supervisors to move their students towards the ultimate goal of being able to study independently in a thoughtful, coherent and efficient manner and is a go-to guide for both novice and experienced supervisors seeking to develop their practice.

Anne Lee is an independent academic, an Honorary Research Fellow at the University of Bristol, UK and was Associate Professor at the University of Stavanger in Norway. There is more about her work at www.drannelee.wordpress.com

Successful Research Projects

A Guide for Postgraduates

Anne Lee

Routledge
Taylor & Francis Group

LONDON AND NEW YORK

First published 2020
by Routledge
2 Park Square, Milton Park, Abingdon, Oxon, OX14 4RN

and by Routledge
52 Vanderbilt Avenue, New York, NY 10017

Routledge is an imprint of the Taylor & Francis Group, an informa business

© 2020 Anne Lee

The right of Anne Lee to be identified as authors of this work
has been asserted by her in accordance with sections 77 and 78
of the Copyright, Designs and Patents Act 1988.

All rights reserved. No part of this book may be reprinted or
reproduced or utilised in any form or by any electronic,
mechanical, or other means, now known or hereafter invented,
including photocopying and recording, or in any information
storage or retrieval system, without permission in writing from
the publishers.

Trademark notice: Product or corporate names may be
trademarks or registered trademarks, and are used only for
identification and explanation without intent to infringe.

British Library Cataloguing-in-Publication Data
A catalogue record for this book is available from the British
Library

Library of Congress Cataloging-in-Publication Data
Names: Lee, Anne, Dr., author.
Title: Successful research projects : a guide for postgraduates /
Anne Lee.
Description: Abingdon, Oxon ; New York : Routledge, 2020. |
Includes bibliographical references.
Identifiers: LCCN 2019001989| ISBN 9780815376743 (hardback)
| ISBN 9780815376750 (pbk.) | ISBN 9781351236188 (ebk.)
Subjects: LCSH: Academic writing–Handbooks, manuals, etc. |
Report writing–Handbooks, manuals, etc. | Universities and
colleges–Graduate work. | Research–Methodology.
Classification: LCC LB2369 .L36 2020 | DDC 808.02–dc23
LC record available at https://lccn.loc.gov/2019001989

ISBN: 978-0-8153-7674-3 (hbk)
ISBN: 978-0-8153-7675-0 (pbk)
ISBN: 978-1-351-23618-8 (ebk)

Typeset in Galliard
by Integra Software Services Pvt. Ltd.

Printed and bound by CPI Group (UK) Ltd, Croydon, CR0 4YY

This book is dedicated to the youngest members of my family: Joshua, Sebastian, Lizzy, Robin and Tessa. May you keep on asking 'why?'

Contents

Figures

Tables

Boxes

Preface

Successful research projects offers a comprehensive, practical, research-based framework for you to be able to examine your practice, solve problems and plan your research effectively. It draws on work from across and between all disciplines and will be useful for scientists, students working in arts and humanities, health care, social sciences and on multi-disciplinary projects.

On a practical level this book aims to help you by:

- collecting together ideas on managing your time
- demonstrating good practice in academic writing
- identifying what help is realistically available to you from your supervisor
- clarifying some of the differences between research projects at undergraduate and postgraduate levels
- listing some of the many other resources you might find helpful
- helping you to keep balanced and flourish throughout the process
- looking at ways to use your research to help your career planning.

It is full of practical examples of best practice gathered from postgraduate students from all over the world.

The time pressures on students doing research have generally increased: there are national and international expectations and more opportunities for data collection, collaboration and generic skills development. The purpose of the book you are now holding in your hand is to provide a neutral language for exploring conceptions, expectations and problem solving – the companion volume is intended to offer the same help for your supervisor so that everyone can plan how to use both their time most efficiently.

Acknowledgements

The feedback from Paul Spencer and Loriel Anderson of Bristol Doctoral College in the UK has made this book complete. Thank you to both of them, to their students and to my other colleagues at the University of Bristol, particularly Professor Sally Barnes and Kate Whittington, with whom I have enjoyed working on our own research project.

Robert Radu and colleagues at the University of Stavanger in Norway have been good friends, supporting many of my initiatives in Norway. Robert's ability to translate my ambitious plans into realistic projects has been wonderful.

I would like to particularly acknowledge the contributions made to the development of the questionnaire by academics from Norway: Shaher Shalfawi from the University of Stavanger and Tor-Ivar Karlsen from the University of Agder and his team. Their interest in the subject has been both helpful and encouraging. We all recognise that there is much more that could be done but steps are being taken in the right direction.

This work began years ago at the University of Surrey. I am deeply grateful to staff and students there. To all the students, academics and supervisors that I have worked with at universities and institutes in the UK, Eire, Scandinavia, mainland Europe, the Middle East and Africa – you have critiqued, extended and examined the thoughts behind this book – thank you.

Many postgraduate students have contributed to this book, starting with my own then a wider group of interviewees at the University of Surrey where I then worked. Now the text reflects contributions from researchers all over the globe. You are the most exciting and dedicated group of people – thank you for all the contributions to improving our world that your research is underpinning.

My aim has been to make this book, and its companion (*Successful Research Supervision*, 2nd ed.) as complete a resource as possible. So I am grateful to Taylor and Francis for letting me include work from the following previously published sources: Lee, A, 'Setting up frameworks' (Chapter 4) and 'Five approaches to supporting students writing in English as an Additional Language' (Chapter 13), in Carter, S. and Laurs, D. (Eds.) (2018) *Developing research writing*, Routledge: Abingdon; Lee, A. (Chapter 1, Chapter 9) in Carter, S. and Laurs, D. (2014)

Developing generic support for doctoral supervisors, Routledge: Abingdon; Lee, A. & Murray, R. (2015) Supervising writing: Helping postgraduate students develop as researchers, *Innovations in Education and Teaching International*, 52(5), 558–570; and Lee, A. (2018) How can we develop supervisors for the modern doctorate? *Studies in Higher Education*, 43(5), 878–890.

I am also grateful to Vitae.ac.uk for granting permission to reproduce the Researcher Development Framework at the RDF Enterprise Lens.

A note on terminology

Words that are used interchangeably

Postgraduate research student, doctoral candidate or early career researcher?

A doctoral candidate in Europe is often called an 'early career researcher' (ECR) – an important statement about identity and one possible career trajectory. In other countries the term 'Early Career Researcher' refers to the student who has already been awarded their PhD (the post-doc). In this book the terms 'research student', 'researcher' and 'ECR' are used interchangeably to refer to someone doing postgraduate research at either master's or doctoral level and in some cases the principles can apply to a student undertaking an ambitious research project at undergraduate level. Post-docs are often involved in some supervision of students doing research, so they will also have an interest in this book.

Dissertation or thesis?

In the UK 'dissertation' is usually applied to an extensive piece of research submitted for a master's or undergraduate degree. 'Thesis' is used to describe a monograph, or an extended piece of research at PhD level. The terms 'dissertation' and 'thesis' are used to describe exactly the opposite levels of research in higher education in the USA and elsewhere. In this book, both terms are used to describe an extended and rigorous piece of original research.

Advisor or supervisor?

The terms 'supervisor', 'academic' and 'advisor' are used interchangeably in this book. In North America the phrase 'advisor' is more common; in the UK and Australia 'supervisor' is generally used.

Mentoring or coaching?

Mentoring in this book is used to describe a holistic process, largely non-directive facilitation. Coaching is more skills based, where the coach has a good idea of the expertise that needs to be mastered. So 'mentoring' might include helping to find a range of options for careers, whereas 'coaching' might refer to help with using a particular piece of equipment for an experiment.

Abbreviations

CGS	Council for Graduate Schools (US)
EAL	English as an Additional Language
EdD	Doctorate of Education
EHEA	European Higher Education Area
EngD	Doctorate in Engineering
EUA	European Universities Association
MOOC	Massive Online Open Course
OECD	Organisation for Economic Co-operation and Development
PRIDE	Association of Professionals in Doctoral Education
PsyD	Doctorate in Psychology
QAA	UK Quality Assurance Agency
SEDA	Staff Education and Development Association (a UK-based professional association)
SOTL	Scholarship of Teaching and Learning
SRHE	Society for Research in Higher Education
UKCGE	United Kingdom Council for Graduate Education

Chapter 1

Becoming a research student

Why is this book unique?

The framework that underpins this book seeks to support postgraduates doing research by explaining the different approaches that you can choose from and blend together in order to be successful. I created it from an iterative research study looking at the behaviours and beliefs of effective postgraduate students and their supervisors, interpreted through a wide literature review. It can explain why your supervisors are asking you to undertake certain tasks and what lies behind some of the feedback they may be trying to give you. From extensive research with successful postgraduate students and their supervisors I have identified five conceptual ways of looking at your project. Once you have understood these you will have access to an approach to problem solving that you can use both for doing your research and for other life projects.

For most of this book the framework is depicted as a matrix, exploring each of the five approaches in depth. However, understanding how they link together is important to be able to design a holistic experience for undertaking research successfully. In Figure 1.1 I show the five approaches as a Venn diagram within the overarching functional framework. The functional framework includes the university regulations and project management tools without which no degree can be awarded. Enculturation refers to becoming a welcome member of the department; critical thinking refers to the analytical skills needed to depict and create knowledge; emancipation refers to the ability to make knowledgeable choices; and relationship development covers how to have good relationships with colleagues and supervisors. This book will help you master all of these approaches.

Chapter 2 helps you to understand the framework. Appendix 2 provides more detail about the theoretical base and the research behind it.

So you want to do some research? You want to do it well, probably as easily as possible and definitely within the time limitss you have set yourself.

On a practical level this book aims to help you by:

- collecting together ideas on managing your time
- demonstrating good practice in academic writing

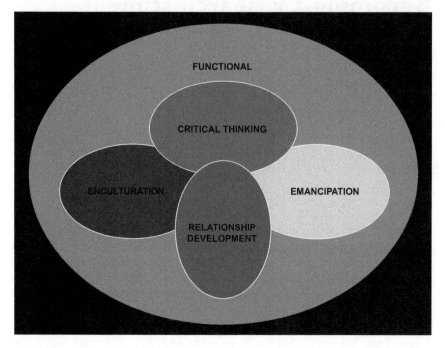

Figure 1.1 A map of the framework demonstrating the inter-relationships

- identifying what help is realistically available to you from your supervisor
- clarifying some of the differences between research projects at undergraduate and postgraduate levels
- listing some of the many other resources you might find helpful
- helping you to keep balanced and flourish throughout the process
- looking at ways to use your research to help your career planning.

How to use this book

If you are new to research, consider starting on Tasks 1–3 in Chapter 3. Reading this book from beginning to end in one go could give you intellectual indigestion. It is the product of over 20 years' experience of being a research student, a supervisor and leading workshops for research students and supervisors. Scan the contents page for the sections you need now.

It is deliberately structured with lots of subheadings so that you can dip in and out of it as time goes by and according to the size of research project you are undertaking. For example, Chapter 3 is a good place for most people to start, but you may not want to read the section in Chapter 4 on 'how do disciplines think' until you are well into your research project.

If you are facing specific problems, look at the subheadings to see if any of them might include some helpful suggestions for you.

If you have any teaching responsibilities, or are coming from an education system that does not operate within the European Higher Education Area (EHEA) framework, you will find it helpful to identify some of the differences in doing research at undergraduate and postgraduate levels. You will find examples relating to research at different levels throughout the book.

How to make the effort of undertaking a research project worthwhile

A researcher is someone who can make a reasoned step into the unknown.

You may have *intrinsic* reasons for wanting to do research (perhaps a deeply held desire to uncover information and create new knowledge about a particular phenomenon), or *extrinsic* reasons (for example, a qualification to get a job). Either or both are fine, but understanding your motivation(s) for undertaking this project will help you to keep going if you find yourself getting confused by the amount of information you unearth (a common feeling, and an important stage to work through, because clarity will follow).

In this next section I explore what doing research means at different levels of higher education. It is important to get some feel for this because you may have done research as an undergraduate or master's student and want to be clear about how to define the difference between your previous experience and the next level up. The following descriptions are taken from the European Higher Education Area's 2018 publication of a Higher Education Qualifications Framework. At the time of writing there are 48 members and partners of the EHEA from Europe and beyond.

At the undergraduate bachelor's level, students doing research have to demonstrate knowledge and understanding in a field of study that builds upon what is available in advanced textbooks, solve problems and create arguments that can be sustained by gathering relevant data. At master's level, there is an additional requirement to be able to apply problem-solving techniques in new and unfamiliar environments and be able to form judgements with incomplete or limited information. At doctoral level there is an expectation that you will have made an original contribution that extends the frontier of knowledge. At every level there is an expectation that students are aware of social and ethical responsibilities. (These descriptions are abstracted from the EHEA Qualifications Framework, summarised in Table 1.1 at the end of the chapter.)

We know that all qualified researchers have important skills for life and are sought by employers. Doctoral graduates make a substantial contribution to business, academia, government, community, not-for-profit sectors and academia (Bryan & Guccione, 2018). We also know that doing research well is very hard work. Is doing any form of research going to be worth it for you?

I (Anne, the author) start from a biased position. I think that doing your own research offers the most wonderful opportunities. From smaller projects that give you licence to ask questions and gather material, to having an opportunity to be the person who knows the most about your topic and the ability to contribute original knowledge at a doctoral level, having good research skills enables us to learn how to start into something new.

At an undergraduate and master's levels there may be no escape from your tutor's expectations. The obligation to undertake a research project or write a dissertation is written into the curriculum of many courses, so if you want the qualification you will have to do it. The secret is to find a topic that is both meaningful and useful to you and achievable. At a doctoral level, it is what you have volunteered for. So the better question is 'how can I make it worth it for me?'

Identifying the risks to be avoided

1   **Failing to use research to plan your career.** The financial advantages to your career of doing a master's degree are clear, especially for women. Post-doctoral earning is not guaranteed but employment opportunities do generally increase with qualification (Casey, 2009). So it is vital to choose work on the most appropriate research question and use it to explore career options and create networks from the beginning. Even if you do not yet know what you want to do with the rest of your life, developing research skills and exploring all avenues will help you find out.

2   **Not planning to maintain both mental and physical health.** This has rightly gained a much greater public profile recently. How can we make sure that you are in the healthy 68 per cent of PhD students who (from a Belgian sample) avoided the risk of developing common psychiatric disorders (Levecque, Anseel, De Beuckelaer, Van der Heyden, & Gisle, 2017). Mental health is variously defined as the ability to work productively, maintain effective relationships and overcome adversity (Vailes, 2017, p. 26). It is important to plan to maintain some physical activity, healthy eating, social support, holiday and vacation breaks.

3   **Inadequate or confusing supervision.** Much of this book is aimed at helping you to get the best out of your supervisor(s), using the limited time you may have together to your advantage. Reports of toxic relationships with supervisors are thankfully in the minority, but if you find yourself in such a relationship turn to Chapter 10. The greatest risk comes from simply not being able to understand what the supervisor is trying to say or do. Decoding your supervision sessions is a key part of getting the most out of the precious time you have together and the framework introduced in Chapter 2 is intended to help you with this.

Maximising the benefits

Having said that there is no guaranteed career arising from doing research, interviews with doctoral graduates indicated that many did see advantages to their career development some five years after completion. Bryan and Guccione (2018) cite several examples (especially from STEM subjects) where their interviewees were certain that the research qualification they obtained was essential in them getting jobs and accessing consultancy work that would not have otherwise been open to them.

All their interviewees recognised that they had developed significant useful skills through doing their research, the most significant of which were abstract cognitive skills including critical thinking. This means that it is very important to be able to describe these skills in a way that employers will find compelling. Undertaking work placements is seen as an important avenue to be able to do this.

Being part of an active and supportive group or department can enhance a feeling of well-being and self-esteem, wherever you are. At its best, working within a group whose members have been recruited specifically for their intellectual skills offers an exciting environment that it is difficult to find the equivalent of elsewhere. Self-esteem is different to status. While students may start a course to get the qualification and post-nominals, it is rarely the title that is the most important element as time goes by. The feeling of achievement when a piece of work is submitted can be close to elation (even more when the assessment results are positive). At a doctoral level, it is a particularly hard-won feeling of elation and should be enjoyed. The increased self-confidence that comes from overcoming challenges and from having made strong working relationships, as Bryan and Guccione argue, is an invaluable, life-enhancing attribute.

Choosing where and with whom to do your research

If you have not yet chosen a university, research institute or supervisor to work with, then start reading here.

The university you go to may open doors to careers that you had not thought of, so close reading about any employment links and placements they organise, as well as looking at careers that their alumni have undertaken, is necessary.

If you are seeking an academic career then it's sensible to aim for a university that has a history of sending its graduates to work in other universities. If you want to stay local then choose a university that is embedded in its region. Interesting clues to a university's employability records and strengths abound in unusual places – has the university chosen a local person as its Chair, Provost, President, Chancellor or Rector, or has it looked for a more national or international figure? (These are ceremonial roles but also can have a key influence in the overall direction of a university because in addition to handing out degrees at graduation ceremonies, they frequently chair important meetings.) Which aspect of different league tables does your preferred university highlight and what does it not say? What does its website highlight about the university strategy or key objectives? Is it focusing on particular industry, business and/or public sector employers or does it describe many multi-disciplinary projects (sometimes known as 'The Grand Challenges'). If you want to travel and learn another language, this is an ideal opportunity and very worthwhile, but expect a few challenges on the way. In any case, you still need to look at what the alumni have gone on to do.

There are a number of international differences between PhD programmes. In the USA you will join a taught programme and only have an individual supervisor (or supervisory team) after a couple of years. In much of Scandinavia the supervisor is not allowed to be involved in the recruitment process (to avoid bias), but positions in places like Norway and the Netherlands are often remunerated full-time employee roles, with pension. In other countries there are varying fee levels and sponsorship might come with quite a few obligations – for example, the obligation to go back to a home country and work there for many years after graduation, or to teach a course as part of a longer degree programme.

The evolution of the doctorate from being primarily a licence to teach in the Middle Ages, through its role in the nineteenth-century university as a centre of research, to the more homogenised and capitalised product that we have today, has been well charted (Taylor, Kiley & Humphrey, 2018). The clever student recognises that the current formalisation of introducing research into the curriculum, especially the doctorate, has led to larger numbers of students, more competition and different measures of success (metrics), especially measuring the number of successful completions on time. This inevitably impacts on institutional expectations of students, but the clever student also seizes every new opportunity to maximise their chances of doing the type of research they truly want to undertake.

In the UK you will have the choice of undertaking a traditional PhD by research (see Figure 1.2) or a professional doctorate. The professional doctorate (such as the EdD in education, DBA in business, PsyD in psychology and EngD in engineering) will often have more taught and assessed courses and may have a slightly shorter research project, but in some cases goes alongside a licence to practice in a particular profession (see Figure 1.3). These are sometimes referred to as 'modern doctorates' and they have closer links with employability outside academic (see www.superprofdoc.eu for case studies on different programmes across Europe). There are opportunities to undertake a PhD by publication (where esteemed published articles and sometimes books form the main part of the thesis but the capstone document that pulls them all together is very important; see Figure 1.4). The PhD by publication is sometimes a route open to existing, experienced members of academic staff.

If you are at the stage when you know exactly what area you want to research in then you need to meet possible supervisors and academics before

Long, thin: focused piece of research
(monography)

Figure 1.2 Shapes of the doctorate (1): the deep, narrow research-question-oriented doctorate

Funnel: demonstrating mastery of
the field (sometimes assessed
modules) and a research project

Figure 1.3 Shapes of the doctorate (2): the funnel – a doctoral programme where broad mastery and research depth are both required

Capstone: PhD by publication with a
'capstone', a document
that pulls together previously
published research

Figure 1.4 Shapes of the doctorate (3): the PhD by publication with a capstone document

committing to that group. In some countries and for some programmes you apply to (or through) a named academic. Occasionally, researchers have found to their cost that choosing a high-profile academic as their supervisor has meant that their supervisor is incredibly busy, travels a great deal and has very little time for face-to-face meetings, so asking how much time a supervisor is likely to have to spend with you at this interview stage could give you very helpful information.

First stages in career planning

Background on careers for PhD graduates

After achieving a doctorate or a post-doctoral contract, an academic career or other role in higher education may seem the most obvious next step in a PhD graduate's career. In Norway a recent report suggested that 60 per cent of PhD graduates want an academic/research career (Reymert, 2017). In the UK the Postgraduate Research Experience Survey (PRES) (2017) reported that 39 per cent want an academic career in higher education and 14 per cent want a research career in higher education, while 15 per cent were not sure yet. Other career aspirations that between them made up about 20 per cent of the sample were: any other professional career; 'the employer who is sponsoring the degree'; self-employment and teaching. There were over 57,000 participants in the survey from 117 UK universities, 65 per cent UK residents, 9 per cent EU and 26 per cent non-EU (Slight, 2017).

However, the ambition of up to 60 per cent of PhD graduates to follow an academic career is often not happening in practice. Hunt, Jagger, Metcalfe and Pollard (2010) found that only a minority of doctoral graduates (19 per cent) work in higher education research roles three and a half years after graduating and 22 per cent in higher education (HE) teaching or lecturing. Most of the rest have moved into roles outside HE in sectors such as healthcare, education, engineering and business.

There are many different influences behind the careers choices made by doctoral candidates. An Australian review identified a range of factors including: work experience, whether or not the qualification was obtained at a research-intensive university, distance learning, the use of certain job search strategies and access to networking opportunities (Jackson & Michelson, 2015).

Another key influence to take into account is how individuals see their identity trajectory. The power of the 'imagined future' is very strong and explored by McAlpine and Turner (2012).

How career aspirations develop

According to a publication by Vitae (Haynes, Metcalfe & Yilmaz, 2016), the long-term career aspirations of respondents changed significantly if they had subsequently been employed in higher education doing research:

- Only 18 per cent continued to have aspirations for an academic career.
- The most common career aspiration was for a non-research career outside HE, selected by one-third of respondents.
- Aspirations to self-employment/running own business/consultancy or other role in HE both more than quadrupled to around one-fifth of all respondents.

Male respondents were slightly more likely to report an aspiration to a career in research, both within HE and other sectors. Females were twice more likely than males to report aspirations of a long-term career in HE in roles other than research and/or teaching. Overall, long-term aspirations showed a more even spread of career interests and were fluid, with movement in various directions. For example:

- a significant number of respondents aspired to further career transitions, for example one-fifth aspired to self-employment/running own business or consultancy, double those currently self-employed
- only 70 per cent of those who now aspired to a research career in HE held that aspiration as HE research staff
- only 40 per cent of those who now aspired to a research career outside HE were the same individuals who had held that aspiration as HE research staff.

Imagined future selves

At the beginning of this chapter, the first risk mentioned was 'failing to use research to plan your career'. One of the ways to counter this risk is to look at all those you meet during your research and build up a picture of the type of work they are doing. Our identity is formed in complex ways, and is constantly evolving, so it can be powerful to imagine ourselves undertaking various roles in the future (McAlpine & Turner, 2011). As that exploration deepens, so we can make more reasoned decisions about whether or not this is the future we seek. Chapter 12 explores ways of doing that.

Possible occupations

Of those surveyed by Haynes et al. in 2016, four-fifths of those in work were employed in one of nine occupations (see also Chapter 12). When starting as a student doing research it is important to consider the broadest possible range of roles and organisations. In some countries commercial organisations will offer more opportunities to do pure research than might be available in academic institutions, but these opportunities may also be directed by commercial objectives. As we will see, the transferable skills gained through doing research can open a wide range of career options in commercial, public sector and not-for-profit institutions. There are also many levels of education and many ways of working in education to be considered – from policy to practice. A growing group, for example, are the researcher developers.

While most PhD graduates in Norway are employed, even there there is still, as elsewhere, a problem with short-term contracts (Thune, Kyvik, Olsen, Vabo & Tomte, 2012). In the UK the Concordat on Careers (Vitae, 2008) aims to create a more stable environment for academic researchers by influencing funders and employers. In a fast-moving world looking to the past is not always the best guide to the future, which is why in Chapter 12 there is also a section on the entrepreneurial researcher.

Longer-term trends

Trends in longer-term employment for doctoral graduates have been measured three years from graduation. This research highlighted the major value of doctoral study to researchers, employers and society. There was good evidence for the relative employability and value of doctoral graduates and it identified an earnings premium for those with a PhD over those with a master's degree but warned against the economic insecurity caused by short- and fixed-term post-doctoral contracts (Mellors-Bourne, Metcalfe & Pollard, 2013).

Summary of advice on career planning as you start your research

1   Choose a research topic that will introduce you to the broadest possible network of people so you can see how and where they work and decide whether or not it is for you.
2   Use your developing research skills to find out about and keep records on jobs and organisations that you find interesting.
3   Keep as many options open as possible: if you are offered (or create) the opportunity to publish from or present your research, even if it doesn't seem important at the time, do it because it will keep open doors that might later become attractive, Moreover, it is a positive thing to put on your CV. Imagine yourself in as many roles as possible to create a range of 'possible selves'.

What can you expect from your supervisor?

This varies depending upon your needs, their strengths and how the university is organised. In some universities there are now large generic undergraduate and postgraduate support programmes. These can include outstanding help with writing academic English and writing English as an additional language. Some universities are organised so that they have good postgraduates or post-docs trained to offer disciplinary-based help in such things as data search, statistics and other quantitative and qualitative methods of analysis. Team building, project management and communication skills are also often on offer. Many universities have outstanding work placement or work experience plans and excellent careers departments, so your supervisor's role might be to highlight these opportunities and enable you to access them. The framework introduced in Chapter 2 and which runs throughout the rest of this book is one way of analysing what you need (and this will change at different stages of your research) and the concepts of supervising research that your supervisors may be operating from. Then you can identify strengths, any gaps and discuss how these gaps might be filled.

The European Higher Education Qualifications Framework

There are many excellent national frameworks of higher education which set out in outline what is expected of students at different levels (see examples for

Table 1.1 Extract from the EHEA Framework of Qualifications (2018)

First Cycle (BA Hons) KNOWLEDGE	Second Cycle (Master's) KNOWLEDGE	Third Cycle (PhD) KNOWLEDGE
Students:	Students:	Students:
• have demonstrated knowledge and understanding in a field of study that builds upon their general secondary education, and is typically at a level that, whilst supported by advanced textbooks, includes some aspects that will be informed by knowledge of the forefront of their field of study • can apply their knowledge and understanding in a manner that indicates a professional approach to their work or vocation, and have competences typically demonstrated through devising and sustaining arguments and solving problems within their field of study • have the ability to gather and interpret relevant data (usually within their field of study) to inform judgements that include reflection on relevant social, scientific or ethical issues	• have demonstrated knowledge and understanding that is founded upon and extends and/or enhances that typically associated with the first cycle, and that provides a basis or opportunity for originality in developing and/or applying ideas, often within a research context • can apply their knowledge and understanding, and problem-solving abilities in new or unfamiliar environments within broader (or multidisciplinary) contexts related to their field of study • have the ability to integrate knowledge and handle complexity, and formulate judgements with incomplete or limited information, including reflecting on social and ethical responsibilities linked to the application of their knowledge and judgements	• have demonstrated a systematic understanding of a field of study and mastery of the skills and methods of research associated with that field • have demonstrated the ability to conceive, design, implement and adapt a substantial process of research with scholarly integrity • have made a contribution through original research that extends the frontier of knowledge by developing a substantial body of work, some of which merits national or international refereed publication • are capable of critical analysis, evaluation and synthesis of new and complex ideas

(Continued)

Table 1.1 (Cont).

COMMUNICATION	COMMUNICATION	COMMUNICATION
• can communicate information, ideas, problems and solutions to both specialist and non-specialist audiences	• can communicate their conclusions, and the knowledge and rationale underpinning these, to specialist and non-specialist audiences clearly and unambiguously	• can communicate with their peers, the larger scholarly community and with society in general about their areas of expertise
CONTINUOUS LEARNING	**CONTINUOUS LEARNING**	**CONTINUOUS LEARNING**
• have developed those learning skills that are necessary for them to continue to undertake further study with a high degree of autonomy.	• have the learning skills to allow them to continue to study in a manner that may be largely self-directed or autonomous.	• can be expected to be able to promote, within academic and professional contexts, technological, social or cultural advancement in a knowledge based society.
Normally includes 180–240 ECTS credits	*Normally carries 90–120 ECTS credits – the minimum requirements should amount to 60 ECTS credits at the Second Cycle level*	*ECTS credits not specified*

Source: Adapted from the EHEA Framework (2018).
www.ehea.info/media.ehea.info/file/2018_Paris/77/8/EHEAParis2018_Communique_AppendixIII_952778.pdf

Ireland: www.qqi.ie/Articles/Pages/National-Framework-of-Qualifications-(NFQ).aspx; the UK: www.qaa.ac.uk/docs/qaa/quality-code/qualifications-frameworks.pdf (2014); Norway: www.nokut.no/en/norwegian-education/the-norwegian-qualifications-framework-for-lifelong-learning/; and Australia www.aqf.edu.au/aqf-levels). It is worth delving into the part of the one that is most relevant to you. Perhaps the most commonly used one was originally devised at Bologna for the European Higher Education Area, and in the abstraction created for Table 1.1 we can see some differences between the different levels of the curriculum laid out next to each other. Here we can see that the first section for each level of knowledge relates to the level of understanding of knowledge that is required; the second section relates to the ability to continue their learning; and the third section relates to the student's ability to communicate that knowledge. The EHEA Framework of Qualifications is the set of descriptors which covers the widest higher education area, so that is what is referred to in the following three sections and summarised in Table 1.1.

In this chapter I have deliberately foregrounded some issues about career planning. Not because you need to decide now, but because you need to keep open the widest range of choices available. In Chapter 12 we will look at how to make decisions between these options. But first, in the next chapter I am going to introduce a framework for analysing what you need and what your supervisor (or supervisory team) can offer. This is a problem-solving framework that can be applied to all levels of higher education and many other dilemmas in life, but it originally came out of research into effective supervision with doctoral students and supervisors.

A framework for analysing different approaches to doing research

The framework introduced in this chapter is intended first of all to enable you, the student, to analyse your own preferences, needs, strengths and areas for development. The aim is to use the resources and contacts within your university to work towards becoming an independent researcher. It is only a guide and the five approaches are not quite as discrete as the tables make them appear at first. It is in blending them together that they provide a powerful approach to problem solving. Many hundreds of academics and researchers have now found the framework a useful tool to analyse their own progress and to understand when others around them might most usefully provide help and support.

In outline the framework suggests that students want and need different things, and that these different aspects of support will probably change as the research progresses. The derivation of the framework is discussed in the companion volume *Successful Research Supervision*, but in brief it arose from interviews, focus groups and workshops with both students and supervisors whom students and academic colleagues identified as successful. The sample was drawn mainly from students and academics in the UK, mainland Europe, Scandinavia and the USA, but has included working with colleagues over the years in Australasia.

An outline of the framework showing the summary of the range of needs that students can have is shown in Figure 2.1. Here we can see that the functional needs related to certainty, time management, understanding milestones and wanting clear signposts about what to do next. The enculturation needs relate to a need to belong to the research group, the department or the discipline, and a need to know how to work effectively in this environment (often through learning by observing role models). Critical thinking needs relate to the need to know how to create a strong argument, one that will withstand opposition. Emancipation relates to the need to be self-aware, able to make decisions for ourselves and by ourselves, to fulfil our potential and work at our best (self-actualisation) and relationship needs relate to the need for friendship, empathy, a feeling of being valued and valuable. This implies a mixture of emotional intelligence, being treated equally and nurtured.

Table 2.1 What might students be seeking?

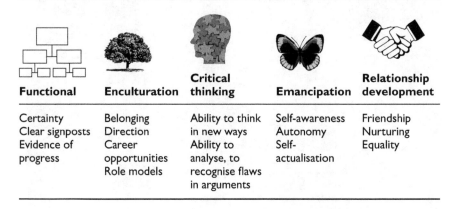

Functional	Enculturation	Critical thinking	Emancipation	Relationship development
Certainty	Belonging	Ability to think	Self-awareness	Friendship
Clear signposts	Direction	in new ways	Autonomy	Nurturing
Evidence of	Career	Ability to	Self-	Equality
progress	opportunities	analyse, to	actualisation	
	Role models	recognise flaws		
		in arguments		

Already we can see that this is a demanding list of expectations, but my aim throughout this book is to empower you to clarify these expectations, to work out which are most important for you, and then to find ways of meeting them while you are doing your research.

The framework is shown as a matrix throughout the rest of this book. In practice the boundaries are fuzzy and for ease of analysis it is perhaps better represented as the Venn diagram shown in Chapter 1 and repeated here with images (Figure 2.1). The overarching frame is the functional approach, even though I warn against over-emphasising the functional approach, I recognise that without an organisational framework there can be no accredited qualifications awarded.

Which are the most important approaches to doing research for you?

This will change over time so be aware that however you answer the questionnaire that follows now, your responses might (and probably should) change as the research progresses. Bearing in mind the limitations of this framework, some people still find a self-assessment tool useful for understanding the different approaches. Below is a questionnaire (Table 2.2) which encourages students and candidates to think about their priorities in the research process. To complete it, tick the box that most indicates how important each issue is to you, and then score it as indicated below.

Understanding your score

This brief questionnaire is designed to help students look at priorities and understand a little more about each of the conceptual approaches to research. It is not (yet) a fully validated instrument, so use it as a guide only.

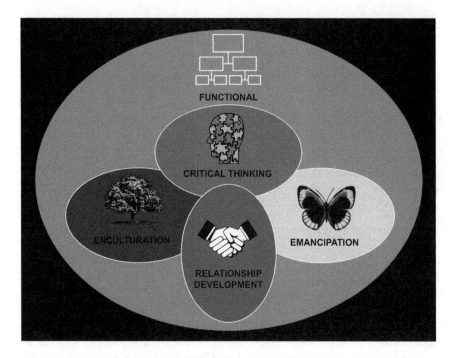

Figure 2.1 A map of the framework demonstrating the inter-relationships

A common pattern is for students who are achievement-oriented to be driven by external deadlines initially, for example, for transfer or annual reports (a functional approach). As time moves on they may extend their interests into discovering more about how things are done successfully in their field or discipline (enculturation). The research process requires developing skills in intellectual rigour and analysis, and for some students developing these thinking skills is the most important aspect of their work (critical thinking). Students who see the research process as a journey of self-discovery as well as intellectual growth and enquiry may find that their intrinsic motivation propels them along new paths and into unforeseen careers (emancipation). For some students and supervisors, the most important element is that they are in a professional relationship where there is integrity and trust (relationships).

Students can use this questionnaire to compare their answers with those of their supervisors and fellow students, to understand why their supervisor might be acting in a certain way and to articulate more clearly what type of support they might find helpful.

Table 2.2 Student's version: a questionnaire and score sheet to enable greater understanding of the framework of approaches to research as a student

Different approaches to doctoral studies

Place one tick in a box on each line to indicate the level of importance you attach to that item.	Unimportant			Important	
	1	2	3	4	5
1. I always like to have a date arranged for the next meeting before I leave the current session					
2. It is important that I know how to design and carry out a project that members of this discipline will recognise as an example of ethical and good practice					
3. It is important to be able to think critically, always to recognise flaws in articles, arguments or work that I see					
4. It is important that I understand what motivates me and I question why I am doing this research					
5. I think I manage my own and others' emotions appropriately					
6. I keep copies of records of each meeting with my supervisor					
7. I want to continue working in this discipline when I have finished my studies					
8. I want to demonstrate an independence of mind					
9. I expect to become a different person, to be changed or transformed by the research work I am doing					
10. I enjoy the time I spend with my research supervisor and other students					
11. I like to send my supervisor something to read before I meet with them, to demonstrate I am making progress					
12. It is important that I understand the work of key researchers in my field					
13. It is important that I am able to put forward counter-arguments to propositions					
14. I may go through periods of self-doubt, a 'dark night of the soul', while doing my research, but I will emerge the stronger for it					

(Continued)

Table 2.2 (Cont.)

Different approaches to doctoral studies

Place one tick in a box on each line to indicate the level of importance you attach to that item.

	Unimportant			Important	
	1	2	3	4	5
15. It is important that I maintain positive working relationships with other departmental staff and help them as required					
16. I note in my diary key dates for annual reports etc., so I can monitor my progress					
17. I look for examples of interesting and excellent work in my field to emulate					
18. I believe that successful researchers are able to think in a broad or interdisciplinary way					
19. I think it is important to learn to reframe the important questions					
20. I can enthuse others by my interest in my work					

Scoring your profile

Add the scores up for the following numbers – it will give you some idea of your priorities as a doctoral student:

Q. no.	Score	Q. no.	Score	Q. no.	Score	Q. no.	Score	Q. no.	Score
1		2		3		4		5	
6		7		8		9		10	
11		12		13		14		15	
16		17		18		19		20	
Total function score		Total enculturation score		Total critical thinking score		Total emancipation score		Total relationships score	

Source: Adapted after Shalfawi (2016) and from Lee (2008)

Table 2.3 Identifying, prioritising and analysing the difficult questions that can arise for students during a research project

These statements have been taken from comments made by students in difficulties.
No one student will face all these difficulties, but putting them all together helps us to identify the most important.

	Is this urgent? Yes/No	Is this important? High, medium, low?	Some avenues for further investigation
Functional			
1 What are the exact systematic steps of doing research?			Gantt charts, work plans, setting shorter-term objectives
2 How do I manage time when I have a busy part-time job and no sense of direction for my research? Time always seems to be chasing me.			Focus on research direction first, then find help with time management
3 It is noisy and there is no space to study where I live.			There will be study space somewhere in the university. Negotiate for or find it
4 I am in serious debt and it worries me.			Student financial advice service
5 My project needs more funding.			Explore all options in detail, cost alternatives then discuss with the supervisor
6 What are the learning objectives for a doctorate? I had handbooks with them clearly set out for my undergraduate and master's degree.			Use the EHEA framework (Table 1.1) or national quality agencies frameworks as a start
7 What do I do if my supervisor leaves the university?			Identify the person/people who are responsible for finding alternatives. This might be co-supervisors, heads of department or post-graduate coordinators. The graduate or postgraduate administrator should help

(Continued)

Table 2.3 (Cont.)

8	I don't see my supervisor enough, but they said emails also count as supervision.	Explore expectations with your supervisor(s) (see Table 7.5) and plan a timetable for the future

Enculturation

9	How can I become a proper member of the research group?	Find out what timetabled departmental events, seminars, presentations take place and go to them. There are often visiting speakers who are glad of an audience
10	I have no one to talk to because my research is so different to everyone else's.	Students who have started at the same time can often support each other as well, because their research is at similar stages, even though it is on different topics
11	I am a long way from my home, family and friends. How do I start to talk to people here?	Is there a network for international students or an international students' office?
12	How can I decide whether I need an extra supervisor or just some expert advice?	Explore the uncertainties and options
13	Can I expect to get careers advice and good contacts from my supervisor?	Discuss expectations at an early stage

Critical thinking

14	My supervisor seems really reluctant to tell me what to do next and to teach me.	Is it time pressure or is your supervisor encouraging independence?

(Continued)

15	I am angry because I don't know how this works. I just want one solid fact to pin things on.	Learning to cope with uncertainty is hard. Reassurance is importance – this might need external support. Would counselling help?
16	I just get 'fine' and 'move on'. When will I be told my work is really good?	Explore your expectations of feedback. Are there cultural or historic experiences here? How can you describe and articulate what you need? How many places can you get feedback from?

Emancipation

17	I don't know what the instruction 'be more independent' means in practice.	Disaggregate independence and explore it (see Table 8.3)
18	Why do all this work when there probably won't be a job for me at the end of it?	Are you making the best of all contacts available? Can you find more careers support?
19	I don't know if I can do this.	This is a common feeling at various stages. It's an important part of being a researcher to recognise it as a threshold. Concentrate on the next goal, not the longer term. Seek reassurance about the level of support available. This statement needs considerable investigation
20	How much teaching should I do? Can I do? Can I say 'no'?	Review time management and assertiveness skills. What training do you need to be an effective teacher in higher education?

(Continued)

Table 2.3 (Cont.)

21	I want to do well so I say yes to most requests. Now I am wondering if I have taken on more than I should.	Review time management and assertiveness skills
22	How do I keep myself motivated?	It's key to know what motivated you in the first place. Does this still apply?
23	How do I make myself stay focused on the task?	Analyse and discuss the pressures with someone

Relationship development

24	Is my supervisor my father or my prosecutor? Why does he invite us out for drinks and then criticise me?	Separate academic from personal criticism. We make good decisions by anticipating problems. Criticism helps us to do that
25	I attended a workshop called something like 'Managing your supervisor'. Why should I do the managing? Isn't that what they are supposed to do?	'Managing upwards' is a life skill. You want to get the best out of your supervisor, not waste time trying to get something irrelevant or unobtainable
26	I was employed in a senior role before. Now I feel as though I am being treated like a teenager and none of my previous (extensive) knowledge is being used or valued.	Differentiate between academic creation of knowledge and impact. Establish how existing strengths can be used and what academic procedures might add to that

27	How can I be assertive enough to ask for more guidance?	Rehearse the what and how
28	My supervisors seem most interested in publications. I am only getting in the way. How can I manage this?	Is this really true? Is it imposter syndrome (a common academic problem) or do you need to get another supervisor to support you?
29	How do I manage a situation where I get conflicting advice from two (or more) supervisors and funders? How do I work effectively with two supervisors? Should we meet together or separately? How do I manage industrial and academic supervisions?	A lot of planning needs to go into creating an effective supervisory team. Have your team ever met together? Identify and use the expertise that all your supervisors offer, interview them and if necessary reconcile differences for yourself by writing a position paper
30	I ask for feedback on my performance and don't receive any (or it's very brief and I don't know how to respond to it).	Explore and discuss expectations (see Table 7.5). Can you voice record supervision sessions so you can listen back to what is said?

Some real worries?

This list of questions asked by students doing research when they were certain that revealing their anxieties and worries would not affect an assessment of their work. In Table 2.3 the questions were grouped according to the framework with some suggestions for places to begin exploring them. Each question can (and should) be analysed under almost every heading of the framework, so this table is intended to be just a starting prompt to explore the problems that might underlie them. In Chapters 9 and 10 we look at some of these issues in more details. If any of the questions below are important for you now, I suggest you identify the most urgent first and put it on the agenda for your next meeting with your supervisor(s). Then use the rest of this book to look at how to generate possible solutions for any other questions that are really important.

In this chapter I have outlined the framework and offered a way for students to identify what is most important to them. Table 2.3 shows a list of the top 30 challenging questions that real students have asked, grouped under the different approaches. Deal with any urgent issues, then the next stage is to use all the approaches to find the best blend for an answer to any other important questions. Some might be solved with quite a simple discussion; others might take most of the period of research to work out an answer to. No one approach is likely to provide a sufficient answer on its own – you probably need to look in several places. In the next chapter we look in more detail at the functional approach, how it can help us to manage time and monitor progress.

Chapter 3

Managing your project
A functional approach

Managing your research as a project

This piece of research is *your* project. You are in charge. So the first skill is to find out what its outline is supposed to look like. We are not going to look at the topic, as such, for the moment, but focus on how to structure it. Look at Box 3.1. Most academic research projects will follow this type of pattern when written up (but not necessarily in this order).

Box 3.1 Typical outline structure for a written research project

1 Defining the research question
2 Literature survey
3 Identifying the gap in the literature that you are going to address
4 Research methods
5 Data collection
6 Data analysis
7 Conclusions
8 References
9 Abstract (although this comes first in the text, it is usually the last piece to be written)

Each of these brief headings will need planning for, and one of the secrets of not being overwhelmed by the scale of the task is to break it down and then just focus on the next task to be undertaken.

Task 1: Organising your references

There are many types of reference management software programmes available (for example, Mendeley, EndNote, Reference Manager) and you need to find

Table 3.1 Sample headings for managing references

Author and full reference	Key theories/perspectives	Intended audience for piece	Research methods/ type of analysis	Sample	Key finding	Limitations

the one that will suit your discipline and be available for your academic career. Most university libraries offer training in the use of referencing systems and I recommend that you do not open a book or journal until you have established the referencing system you want to use. There are many headings that you can sort references by and if you make notes on what you read as you go, writing up the literature survey becomes a much simpler task. Typical headings might include those shown in Table 3.1.

Task 2: Planning a timetable

Setting up a chart of what you need to do in the time that you have to manage this project is the next most useful thing you can do. This chart is not set in stone – it should be discussed and checked out with all your supervisors, and events will mean that you need to revise it. But it will give you a sense of direction and enable you to know when and if things need adjusting. This chart is intended to help you to work towards producing the document that we outlined in Table 3.1.

Gantt charts were created as an engineering project management tool. They are a graphical illustration of the schedule of the tasks that need to be scheduled and coordinated. They are now widely used in project proposals and as a management tool for planning change to try to turn what is often a very complex endeavour into something feasible and realistic. This is probably the first time you will have had an overview of what needs to be done to complete your research project, and once a first draft of your Gantt chart has been created you should have a great sense of relief that you have embarked upon a manageable task. Taking it with you to an early meeting with your supervisors will mean you can check whether or not it includes the right tasks and allows appropriate time for them to be completed.

A key advantage of drawing up a Gantt chart is that it makes sure you do not create or undertake a project that is too ambitious (or maybe not ambitious enough). One of the questions frequently asked of any piece of research is: 'what size should my sample be?' Different research methods indicate different answers to this question, but the Gantt chart will also help you with this, because one answer is 'how large a sample can I reasonably include in the time that I have to do this project?'

Table 3.2 shows a very simple Gantt chart for a project. It is intended just to give you an outline of the idea. If you are undertaking a three-year research project, you may want to create several Gantt charts, one for the whole three years and then a more detailed one for the upcoming year.

What is a deadline?

One of the first areas we need to look at are deadlines. By when (ideally) should this thesis or dissertation be submitted? You also need to bear in mind, for your career and financial management plans, that submission is still only part of the assessment process and there can be some months between submission and the assessment. Table 3.3 shows a month-by-month version of a short one-year project. You will probably want to do something a bit more detailed. Please note how early this project plans for submission. It does not need to be submitted until August, but the Gantt chart shows the final writing up being completed in June. There are two reasons for doing this: first, it allows contingency time for things to go wrong; second, if it is achieved, it allows you a well-deserved holiday at the end. January is also completely blank for another holiday (although a whole month for that is perhaps rather generous).

If you are finding it daunting to start writing a Gantt chart, you might find it easier to start collecting ideas on a mind map or a snowflake diagram (where you put the research topic centrally and then additional information or questions as they arise in any pattern emanating from that point). Another approach is to create a research noticeboard (see Figure 5.3). The important thing at this stage is to start identifying the tasks that need to be done. Don't expect to complete any list on your own. Discuss your draft with your supervisors and peers to check it out.

Applying for ethics approval

The Gantt chart in Table 3.3 suggests applying for ethics approval in the second month. Applying for such approval can be quite a lengthy process, so checking when the ethics committee meets and what its deadlines are is an important part of this task. However, going through the process itself is usually very helpful because it means that you will have already been guided through quite a lot of the project procedures. For example, if you have to gain informed consent, you will need to provide the paperwork showing how you plan to do that. That will then be an important part of the project done. Similarly, if you are interviewing or organising focus groups, you will have to plan the questions, recording and data storage as part of the ethics application. If

Table 3.2 A simple Gantt chart to plan a one-year project

Task	September	October	November	December	January	February	March	April	May	June	July
Establish referencing	■										
Read literature	■	■	■	■							
Training in research methods		■	■								
Apply for ethics approval		■	■								
Identify sample				■							
Data collection						■	■				
Data analysis							■	■			
Writing up			■	■		■	■	■	■		
Submission										■	

Table 3.3 A sample risk analysis

Type of risk	Probability(p) (1=low 5=high)	Importance(I) (1=low 5=high)	Total P x I	Person responsible	Risk Prevented or managed by
Computer breakdown					
No access to planned sample/ data					
Supervisor withdraw/illness					
Loss of data					
Data results insignificant					

you are carrying out experiments the ethics application will want details of important health and safety requirements. All of these are important parts of planning the project and will probably make you generate some information that will be included in your final thesis.

Advantages of a Gantt chart

- It frees you up from worry about the big project so you can just focus on the next task.
- It provides a document for discussion with your supervisors.
- If one task gets obstructed for a while, you can easily see what else you could usefully be doing.
- It gives you an idea of the size of project you should be aiming for.
- It allows you to have holidays.
- It is a very good idea to schedule in some rewards for yourself when various tasks are achieved.

Task 3: Doing a risk analysis

We want this project to be successful, so it is important to anticipate any possible risks so that they can be minimised. Just as for the Gantt chart, undertaking this exercise produces a document for discussion with your supervisor(s), and that can provide reassurance (for all parties). One version of a sample risk analysis is shown in Table 3.3. The purpose of this tool is to ask 'in how many ways could it go wrong?' It may or may not be important to do the probability exercise, but including the column 'risk prevented or managed by' is vital.

Take good care of your sample

Your sample might be people, interviewees or participants, it might be bacteria on a petri dish, pieces of moon dust, artwork, or data from a computer program. Whatever it is, it is the most important part of your research.

If it is people then negotiating access to them is often more complicated than you might think. Even once they have agreed to participate and signed the ethics agreements, they can withdraw at any time. I have known people withdraw because they became too busy to be involved, they decided they did not trust the researcher, they became ill, they moved job, home or institution. It is always important to recruit far more people than you think you will need, especially if you aim to do any form of repetitive sampling or a longitudinal study. Then it is important to plan how often you intend to keep in contact with them, and to maintain that. In most cases the cynic would argue that people will participate if they think they are going to get something out of doing so. What are they going to get out of participating in your research – feedback on the project, copies of any subsequent publications, introduction to new ideas or resources? They probably need more than just a warm feeling from having helped a research student on their way.

If your sample is material based, a risk analysis becomes paramount. In how many ways could this go wrong? Might the machine break down, the fridge have a power cut? Could a tray of precious items be knocked onto the floor? Wherever possible having duplicate (or even triplicate) sets is important, preferably stored in different locations. If you never need them they can be handed on for someone else to repeat the experiments and thus give your research added credibility.

If your sample is data then working out how you are going to back up every stage of the work is vital. Separate systems and separate locations are a good idea, but sometimes not possible if there are confidentiality or intellectual property issues. In that case it is important to have a conversation with your supervisor about what options there are for ensuring security. Often there is a people element to negotiating access to data, and in that case you need to take as much care over the relationship with the gatekeeper to that data as you do with the data itself.

Managing time

Many universities now offer generic skills courses and workshops on managing time and this can be such a useful skill for life that they are normally recommended. We all have timewasters in our lives such as playing games or dealing with unnecessary emails, but they might also be providing our brains with important temporary relief so managing them and using them as rewards for tasks achieved might be a more useful solution than trying to eliminate them. One of the occupations that in some cultures is regarded as a timewaster (meeting for coffee and a chat) is regarded in another culture as an important social duty. In Sweden, stopping work and going for fika (coffee and a snack) is routine, but they only do it once (or twice) a day, not all the time. So time management does not have to be about denial; it can be about managing rewards.

It is also about managing information. Keeping a list of 'things to do' is a common and useful way of keeping track of what we need to get done each day. Managing emails and social media may also need some attention. How you file your emails will make a difference to how much time they take. Some people use a range of 'completed' files as a way of keeping records, and move new emails that require action or watching to a 'pending' file. Then they can keep their inbox clear. Social media is one of the opportunities that can be managed as a reward.

Meetings with your supervisor(s)

In many universities supervisors are allowed a set number of hours for supervising students doing research. Those hours are normally expected to include reading drafts, replying to emails and face-to-face or Skype meetings. If you have a supervisory team these hours may be divided up or allocated between supervisors. So this resource needs to be carefully used and well planned. In Chapter 7 we look at ways of exploring and understanding what both supervisors and students might expect of each other. Misunderstandings about expectations are often at the bottom of relationship breakdowns. To prevent this and to help your planning, it is a good idea to try to set up a schedule of meetings. Emphasise that this schedule is not a straightjacket, rather it is a plan that can be amended as necessary (with reasonable notice and explanation on both sides). However, if you know how many face-to-face meetings in a year you can expect with your supervisors and how often they would like to meet you as a team, it will help you plan what you want to raise with them.

This becomes both more complex and easier if you have regular lab or research team meetings. Research team meetings will usefully keep you in touch with an overall project, lab procedures and culture, but you still need to understand how many one-to-one meetings you can expect to help with your individual thesis or dissertation.

After every meeting with your supervisors it is a good idea to make a few brief notes and send them to the supervisor so they can see what you have understood as a result of the meeting. Some universities have systems that keep these records online. A basic structure would be to record brief notes about:

- an outline of what was discussed
- what the student is going to do next
- what the supervisor(s) are going to do next
- date of next meeting.

Basic information to keep safe for reference

Your university will have programme handbooks, codes of practice and student agreements. In the flurry of starting a research project it is easy to mislay these. Set aside a file for such information so you can refer to it as necessary. For longer projects you need to know what formal records need to be submitted (often annual reports and upgrade reports). You might want to know what the guidelines are for sickness or maternity/paternity leave or suspension of studies. One day that information on intellectual property, or who owns the data you are generating, might be very important.

Questions for further contemplation

Does your Gantt chart include sufficient time for getting an ethics application passed?

How much time have you allowed for negotiating access to your field or getting your data sample?

Who is/are the gatekeeper(s) to your data? How can you keep them positive towards your research? Can you send short reports or updates to anyone who helps your research?

What 'rewards' are you going to allow yourself for completing both big and little tasks?

What is the outline meetings schedule with your supervisors?

In this chapter we have covered many of the organisational issues that are important in managing a research project. In the next chapter we look at how to understand what is going on in an academic discipline and get involved in the work of the department.

Chapter 4

Uncovering the implicit
Embracing enculturation

Why is enculturation important?

Enculturation is about a sense of belonging, becoming a member of a disciplinary community. *Cognitively*, this is about understanding how to make an argument that this disciplinary community finds persuasive. It is also about assimilating its practices and values. *Socially*, it is about feeling part of a community, moving from being a welcomed observer towards increasingly being able to practise as a member of this discipline would, and eventually to mastery so that you can be a role model to others.

In becoming a member of a discipline, you are consciously or unconsciously developing a new identity. Just as 'imagined futures' are an important part of looking at what careers might suit you (see Chapter 1), so an imagined academic identity is important for helping you to understand how people in this discipline, department or research team think and what they think is important. Understanding and creating your identity as an academic is an important part of the research process.

How do different disciplines think?

Murray (2006) encourages students to identify the different conventions of writing in the disciplines; she suggests that they explore language, how arguments are represented, how the researcher is represented, the structure revealed and the options for style and structure. The Carnegie Initiative on the Doctorate (CID) was a five-year programme started in the USA in 2001. The first question it sought to address was 'what is the purpose of the doctorate?' and the answer it explored was 'stewardship of the disciplines'. The project wanted to map and build these fields of knowledge and it focused on six different disciplines to do this: chemistry, education, English, history, mathematics and neuroscience. These fields were deliberately chosen because they included new and old disciplines and demonstrated variation in a number of other different ways, for example different funding patterns, time to career, attrition rates, scope and structure of dissertation (Golde &

Walker, 2006). Essayists were invited to contribute thoughts on the best way of structuring doctoral education in their field. What follows are some examples of their contributions, but the complete texts are a valuable source and necessary reading for anyone who wants to really study their own disciplinary culture.

CID's work implied a broad definition of the word 'discipline'. There are purists who argue that neuroscience, for example, cannot be a discipline; it is a field of study. For these people a discipline is more akin to an approach to thought. While acknowledging this, for the purpose of this book I will accept a broad definition of the word 'discipline'. I am accepting that 'discipline' is a field of study that has its own sets of problems and questions, knowledge bases and approaches to enquiry.

Even within disciplines, academics will often be expected to take a position and from that position will privilege certain types of knowledge – for example a philosopher might take an ontological position from an existentialist or phenomenological point of view and a scientist might be positivist or relativist.

Throughout the disciplines there are similarities in the methods used to encourage enculturation – for example, doctoral students giving seminars or papers to each other and to members of the department, inviting and organising external speakers to give seminars and attending conferences is common practice. There are differences in whether students are encouraged to co-write with academics or to submit journal articles on their own, but both practices are important in enculturation. Potter argues that disciplinary communities need to be encouraged to aid critical reflection while acknowledging that there are generic principles in the scholarship of teaching and learning (Murray, 2008).

Table 4.1 explores some different traditions in the sciences, English, social sciences, history and languages. It looks at various categories: typical approaches to the literature review, research methods, how research questions are identified and predominant structures. It is incomplete for several reasons, primarily because disciplines and thought processes are always evolving, but it is included here as a prompt to encourage you to think about what is being asked of you in your discipline.

If you want to be able to explore good practice in different disciplines then I recommend reading more about the CID project in its chosen seven different disciplines: the sciences, mathematics, chemistry, neuroscience, education, history and English in Appendix B (Golde & Walker, 2006).

Becoming a member of your discipline

Box 4.1 lists ten different ways that you could explore to move from the outside towards the centre of the 'charmed circle' of your discipline.

Table 4.1 Exploring some traditions in the disciplines: how could you add to this for your discipline?

	Sciences	English	Social sciences, education, policy	History	Languages
Typical approaches to the literature review	An interactive literature review process 1 Initiating the literature review process 2 Selecting a topic 3 Exploring the literature: identifying themes 4 Analysing/interpreting/integrating literature 5 Closing the literature search: reaching saturation 6 Writing the review of literature 7 Evaluating process and product	How is your canon bounded? Why have you chosen these texts?	1 Situate your argument in the literature (this also demonstrates knowledge). 2 What does a systematic review mean to you? 3 What do you consider is the influential/seminal literature in your field? What are the limitations of these? 4 What does this tell us and what does it not tell us? 5 Can you compare and contrast two (or more) articles? 6 How did x get published, get funded and become influential/seminal? 7 How have you decided what to include and exclude in your literature review? How did you decide what is enough? 8 What were the research questions that guided and structured your review?	What does this study contribute to the extant literature on the subject? Secondary sources are used to help contextualise the case study and provide a springboard from which to launch one's own study Need to acknowledge intellectual debts, place our work in the broader literature and be careful to point out prior lacunae or failings that we address	What is the purpose of the literature review, e.g. motivation of language learners, cultural differences, teaching and learning?

(Continued)

Table 4.1 (Cont.)

	Sciences	English	Social sciences, education, policy	History	Languages
Comments on research method	Has to try to solve a problem	Refine or define the critical approach at the intersection of the archives – think about how your project articulates to relations and connections	1 Looking for reasoned argument with evidence not proof – seek to establish a balance of evidence (which might be quantity or understanding discourses, e.g. power) 2 What are the strengths and limitations (and caveats) of your work and how would you address them in the future? 3 What are your biases? What are your cultural expectations about criticality? 4 Whose voice is not being heard? How are different voices represented? 5 What are the strengths and limitations (and caveats) of your work and how would you address them in the future? 6 What is the generalisability of your work?	Mostly simple chronological descriptive work. Theoretical frameworks may be rejected as theory imposed upon evidence and thus distorting the evidence. Little conjecture about causation, the model of economically rational actors remains entrenched. Most look for individual or group agency but also recognise structural constraints Some comparative analysis	Cultural framework and expectations have to be identified, clarified and explicit

How research topic is identified and what frameworks of reference are important	Reflective of the context – able to justify your choices of methods of addressing the question Increasingly part of a larger team research-ing questions set by established teams where they can demonstrate a critical mass and expanding boundaries	How do you bound a critical, historical and literary etc. archive? (How do you select the texts you examine?)	Previously, establishing the research question could take a long time. Increasingly now it is a given topic, applied research as part of a larger team Situate your methodological approach within epistemo-logical frameworks, e.g. constructivism, critical realism, feminism, post-colonialism, critical race theory etc. Reflexive — considering your own subjectivity and therefore your own role in creating this knowledge 7 How many different disciplines have a perspective on your topic/field of study? 8 How does this fit in with the bigger picture – meta analysis?	Often stimulated by new access to primary sources. Is it a case study that reinforces or reputes previous interpretations? Often not aware of other 'voices'	Demonstrate awareness of when they are inside and outside their cultural contexts
Structure	1 Research question 2 Literature review 3 Identify the gap 4 Hypothesis 5 Research method 6 Data analysis 7 Discussion 8 Conclusion	How do you make a logical document, explain transitions?	What is your underlying argument?	Mostly chronological structure, what varies is the span involved	What will your contents page look like?

Box 4.1 Ten ways to become a member of your discipline

1 Read the biographies of significant academics in your discipline; follow them on social media.
2 Ask your supervisor(s) to recommend a couple of recent journal articles they think are particularly good, and examine who these authors refer to.
3 Create or join teams or groups of students who normally work solo.
4 Support others in the department doing something different to you, e.g. if you work on theoretical codes seek ways of getting involved with someone who works on applications.
5 Get involved in inviting quest speakers and organising colloquia.
6 Create your 'list' of essential works to be mastered.
7 Get involved in teaching undergraduates or master's students as a form of studying.
8 Present your work, arguments or papers to colleagues in your own discipline.
9 Present your work, arguments or papers to colleagues from another discipline.
10 Join departmental seminar groups or journal clubs.

Formulating the literature review

An important aspect of enculturation is getting to know the discipline's key authors and arguments. 'How much reading should I do? What should I read and how on earth should I analyse it?' are questions that students legitimately ask, and even supervisors sometimes stumble over answering them.

Following leading academics on social media makes it much easier to make contact with them if you meet them at conferences – you already have a point of contact for initiating a conversation.

How much reading needs to be done does, of course, depend partially on the level at which the research is being carried out and the area of enquiry. At an undergraduate level there will probably be two lists given to all students: the essential and desirable set of references. At the undergraduate level students will probably be encouraged to find at least one or two references of their own.

At master's level there will be increased emphasis on students finding their own reading lists. A core literature list will still need to be provided but it should be made clear early on that this is only the beginning. Nygaard (2017) has a very helpful section in Chapter 4 of her book called 'You are what you read'. She advises on how to identify useful search terms (and at this stage she recommends Google Scholar), then recommends moving on to find the right databases and finally to narrow down search terms by words and time. Her advice at this level is to read perhaps 30–50 articles (Nygaard, 2017, p. 55). Tabulating key findings in terms of date, author, title, topic, research question, sample and main findings is a common way of summarising references (see Chapter 3).

At doctoral level the question 'how much reading is enough?' becomes considerably more complex. Frequently, the researcher will be stumbling around in areas new to both them and their supervisors, and this can cause considerable frustration. What can you reasonably expect from your supervisor when part of your work is to step into the unknown? Nygaard (2017) suggests reading perhaps 150 journal articles for a PhD (p. 55) but this depends very much on the discipline. More useful is her recommendation to recognise when you have reached saturation point when whatever you are reading is not adding to the core arguments you have already identified. Whether or not you have read the 'right' journal articles and books is another complex question: a pithy observation made by Boote (2006) is 'a bibliometic analysis of citation quality in dissertations across multiple universities showed that students from less prestigious doctoral programmes use lower quality and easily accessed references' (p. 28). This sounds like an argument for moving well beyond Google Scholar, but it is also an argument for trying to attend relevant seminars and conferences where you will more easily identify the most important and commonly cited authors and arguments.

Summarising, analysing and conceptualising the literature review

In the last chapter I set out one possible table for keeping your references (Table 3.2). The subheading 'limitations' is an important one to consider – especially for those researching at a doctoral level. At an undergraduate or master's level, summarising the literature review in a coherent logical manner would be a good start.

1   Locating the relevant literature as described in the course material
2   Google search to identify key terms
3   Reading most recent books/articles on chosen topic to identify key authors
4   Summarising each piece read in a table

   a.   Reference
   b.   Type of research (qualitative/quantitative/descriptive etc.)
   c.   Key issues/arguments covered

5   Reviewing and restructuring the table to identify linkages
6   Writing up the key linkages

At a master's level the same stages might be followed, with the researcher encouraged to take more control over selecting the research topic and evaluating the final product. So the list might look like this:

1   Selecting the topic
2   Locating relevant literature on research methods
3   Locating relevant literature on topic
4   Reading most recent books/articles to identify key authors and recent trends
5   Summarising each piece read in a table

    a.   Reference
    b.   Research question
    c.   Sample
    d.   Findings
    e.   Strengths/weaknesses/gaps

6   Identifying saturation point when little new is emerging
7   Reviewing and restructuring the table to identify commonalities and gaps.

At a doctoral level different countries and programmes will have different ideas about the broader field to be covered. As we saw in Chapter 1, different types of research-based doctorates will necessitate mastering either broader or deeper reading lists.

At the doctoral level more coverage and depth will be expected of the literature review. The ability to defend the boundaries of the literature considered, to critically examine, synthesise and conceptualise will be expected. These are some of the questions that might be asked here.

- Does the literature review convince readers that the researcher understands the research methodologies, history, and trajectory of current thinking around the topic?
- What strategies for selecting their literature review did the candidate consider?
- Can the researcher situate key literature on this topic in the wider discipline(s)?
- What synergies, biases and gaps are identified? Who was the literature written for and who was it written by?
- Does the researcher identify complications or implications not previously considered?

Using graphic representations for critical analysis and synthesis

At all levels it can be helpful to consider how to present ideas diagrammatically or pictorially. Venn diagrams, concept maps, forms for summarising key points, tables and charts to summarise and evaluate should all be considered. The Cornell method (devised by Professor Walter Pauk from Cornell University) is another way of making notes (see http://lsc.cornell.edu/wp-content/uploads/2016/10/Cornell-NoteTaking-System.pdf).

Arriving at university as an international student

'Culture' can be defined in many ways, but for our purposes I am defining it in its anthropological sense: referring to customs, kinship, language, social practices and worldview. So 'enculturation' means moving towards first an understanding of, and then second a sense of belonging in a new culture. Students moving to a new country to take their postgraduate studies can acquire cultural capital, in addition to the intellectual capital that is gained through participating in the academic community.

In many cases universities also depend on international students for a significant proportion of their fees revenue. The progress of knowledge generation also requires us to work together globally, and the alternative is the argument of minimalisation and protectionism.

Every country needs international students, and if we are aiming to educate a globally competent postgraduate, international students are an essential resource. It is not uncommon to have an academic from one country supervising a student from a second country, with both working in a third country and neither speaking nor writing their native language.

Studies of international students find that they are used to very different learning environments – some have never experienced seminars and tutorials, others do not understand what is required of an 'essay', and some are used to studying and deeply memorising texts rather than group discussion (Biggs & Tang, 2007; Kember, 2000; Okorocha, 2007). As Wisker (2012) has pointed out, international students may not have done research before within a Western university paradigm, so it can be useful to audit both your research and computing skills and seek support early where necessary. An attitude towards doing 'mutual research' is to develop strong intercultural partnerships and is explored further by the Centre of Applied Linguistics at Warwick (Spencer Oatey & Stadler, 2009).

It is easy to make assumptions about international students and to feel alienated by unfamiliar pedagogical practices. For example, how do you cope in a Western system of critical engagement and debate with your supervisor if your previous educational experience has been to 'receive instructions' and to do anything other than nod and agree with the teacher is poor behaviour?

Another difficult problem can be to learn the skill of critical thinking, to be able to formulate an argument, anticipate complex problems and put them on paper coherently. It is interesting that one student found it very helpful when her supervisor taught her to make arguments one paragraph at a time (Nagata in Ryan & Zuber-Skerritt, 1999).

So how might international students respond to the challenge of becoming a research student in a foreign country? Wisker, Robinson, Trafford, Lilly and Warnes (2003b) suggest that they can resort to overcautious contextualisation and learning behaviours that have been 'safe' in the past because they find it difficult to engage fully with problem solving, reflection and deep study.

It is no longer adequate for international students to go to a language centre for a few hours of remedial tuition. The process of enculturation takes years of one-to-one contact, open minds and hearts, and being a student doing research can provide the ideal environment in which this can happen. International students can rightly complain if they are forced to study their topics from just one perspective, and this need to learn about different perspectives can inform and broaden the research project itself. In the UK, if the student is looking at motivation, as well as studying some traditional Western theorists, there may be a need to bring in other advisers, for example, on Confucian understandings or on what the Islamic Koran or the Buddhist Tipitaka has to say about the topic.

What are the cross-cultural issues for international students doing research?

The main binaries that have emerged from research so far are these: communicating (how we might describe things, whether or not we understand a discussion, how familiar we are with academic writing in the language required and how we both deliver and receive robust criticism). There are also different beliefs about the wisdom of sharing knowledge – some always work in a collaborative mode while others believe competition creates important momentum. Trust in relationships can be built in various ways and we explore this in Chapter 7, but some regard it arising as a consequence of strong personal relationships and others have a more transaction-related orientation ('if we agree on a programme and you produce what has been agreed, I will increase my trust in you'). There are issues around ethical work practices, time management, environmental familiarity, the need for support networks and career planning.

Uncovering patterns and relationships

For the purpose of this chapter these elements are expressed as binaries, but in some ways this risks creating a false dichotomy, so readers are encouraged to use these binaries as a launch pad for a discussion rather than viewing them as absolutes.

Discussing differences

Using Table 4.2 as a prompt for ideas, you can discuss with co-supervisors the issues, experiences and expectations that might be held by new researchers

Table 4.2 A discussion document to explore where there may be cultural differences

	CATEGORY	
Low-context (precise, simple, clear) communication expected (see Meyer 2014a, 2014b)	**COMMUNICATING**	High-context (sophisticated, nuanced, layered, elliptical) communication expected
Student and supervisor can both easily understand what the other is saying	**EASE OF UNDERSTANDING**	Student and/or supervisor struggle to comprehend words, phrases and accents
Student fluent in writing in the language required	**EASE OF WRITING**	Student has to master the language required for writing journal articles/thesis
Direct negative feedback preferred (frank)	**STYLE OF CRITICAL FEEDBACK PREFERRED**	Indirect negative feedback preferred (diplomatic, uses softeners and qualifiers)
Collaborative	**SHARING/CREATING KNOWLEDGE**	Competitive
Consensual, egalitarian, democratic (building agreement)	**EXPECTATIONS OF HIERARCHY**	Top-down, hierarchical (unilateral decisions allowed)
Delivering on agreed tasks	**TRUST CREATED BY**	Sound long-term personal relationships

(Continued)

Table 4.2 (Cont.)

	FAMILIARITY WITH THE ENVIRONMENT	
Used to working with the tasks, type of people, food, transport etc. around		Unused to working with the tasks, people, food, transport etc. around
	TIME MANAGEMENT	
Linear time (deadlines matter and are absolute)		Flexible time (deadlines are aspirational)
	AVAILABILITY OF SUP-PORT NETWORK	
Extensive domestic/social support network available		Little or no domestic/social support network available
	IMPORTANCE OF SUP-PORT NETWORK	
Being a member of social groups will significantly enhance the research experience		Candidate prefers to work on their own or with a few well-regarded individuals
	CAREER PLANNING	
Autonomy over career choices		Career expectations already defined/imposed as part of study
	ETHICS	
Ethical procedures are dictated by the department/ programme		To make ethically sound decisions often requires intense questioning

from different backgrounds. There are many other variables that can be considered and you are encouraged to amend these here and then add your own.

A note on identifying intent

The importance of understanding the intent behind the words used is demonstrated in Table 4.3. The same words mean completely different things depending upon the values espoused by the speaker. If the speaker has a competitive orientation they will seek to withhold information until they deem it has its greatest value. If they have a collaborative orientation they will be sharing information openly and risking making themselves vulnerable because they believe that this will lead to greater trust and better quality work.

Table 4.3 The importance of identifying the intention behind the words

	Competition	Collaboration
I would like to share this with you	I will tell you the most inconsequential part so I can assess what sort of risk you pose to my work.	I want you to look at this, tell me honestly what you think about it and I hope that together we can make it even better.
Shall we agree a timetable for this?	I am not doing anything until I see that I am going to get out of it more than I put in.	Let's share what our strengths are and any restrictions we are facing to see how we can mutually support each other.

Question for further contemplation

What are the key arguments in your discipline? Who are the key authors?

Who is/are the gatekeeper(s) to your data? How can you keep them positive towards you research? Can you send short reports or updates to anyone who helps your research?

What opportunities are there for you to attend seminars, conferences and journal clubs?

How can you engage other students and academics in an open exploratory discussion about cultural differences and similarities?

In this chapter we have explored why it is important to try to belong to your discipline and disciplinary community, and how writing the literature review supports this. We have looked at some of the different ways that disciplines think and finally we raised some of the issues that are faced by international students working in a different culture. In the next chapter we explore critical thinking in more detail.

Chapter 5

Thinking like an academic

Developing criticality

The critical thinking approach: an introduction

The term 'critical thinking' is about developing an ability to understand, critique and create the argument. It is used here to describe the intellectual, philosophical and analytical approaches to problem solving that the student will learn to use.

This approach has four elements:

1   understanding different beliefs about knowledge and an ability to assess statements in relation to those beliefs
2   defining and evaluating the argument in a manner appropriate to the relevant discipline or discipline(s)
3   solving problems in a logical manner
4   reflecting metacognitively on performance.

Different beliefs about knowledge

What does knowledge 'look like' to you? How does knowledge appear? This is a fundamental question to be considered in relation to critical thinking – are there any differences in how knowledge emerges or appears in different disciplines? Figure 5.1 suggests so many overlaps across the disciplines that there is no particular disciplinary pattern. Mathematics was not one of the disciplines studied by Donald and some argue that mathematicians understand knowledge differently because they are working within man-made rules and patterns. Once a mathematical formula is proven, unlike a scientific, artistic or social scientific one, it is not going to be disproven. Some mathematicians argue that at its peak or its edge, their subject becomes an art form and therefore can also be subjectively appreciated. Many students struggle with the notion of conditional and provisional thinking, however at doctoral level, one supervisor observed that 'most students do make the leap from dogmatic to provisional thinking'.

Beliefs about knowledge are an important part of understanding critical thinking. Knowledge can be examined in several ways. These include looking at it as a socially constructed process and/or as an inductive/deductive process (Biggs & Tang, 2007). Propositional and practical knowledge are more recognisable within traditional forms of education, and they can be integrated with two other forms of knowledge – experiential and imaginal (Gregory 2006) – or divided into hard/soft/pure and applied, as Biglan(1973a, 1973b) originally did.

Interviews with academic researchers were analysed to see if there were different ways in which knowledge emerged. Knowledge was seen as having different properties and the sorts of comments that academics made suggested that they saw knowledge as:

- being personally experienced, risky, exciting and transforming
- useful when applied
- constrained by procedures
- controversial, contested and provisional
- emerging
- moving, growing and unbounded
- constructed through dialogue
- can be absolute and verifiable
- different in different contexts, for example in different cultures

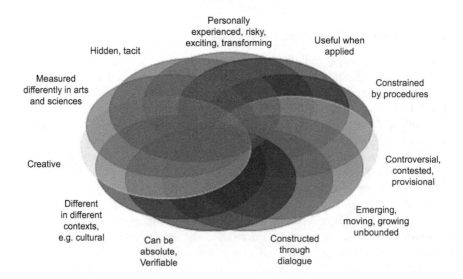

HOW DOES KNOWLEDGE APPEAR IN YOUR SUBJECT?

Results of interviews with doctoral supervisors and students

Figure 5.1 Poster summarising quotations from researchers about knowledge

- creative
- measured differently in arts and sciences
- hidden, tacit, not easy to classify.

These comments were turned into a poster (Figure 5.1) and academic researchers from different disciplines were invited to show how they thought knowledge appeared in their subject. From the excited discussions around the poster, it would appear that further research would be interesting.

If we look behind the concepts that emerged from the discussions we find several key beliefs.

- Knowledge is provisional or absolute (for example 'constructivism' supposes that we create our own knowledge and 'atomism' supposes that knowledge consists of units that are linked to each other).
- Knowledge can be created and constructed.
- There are procedures that constrain the emergence of knowledge.
- Knowledge is sometimes hidden, can be risky and personally transforming.
- Knowledge is different in different contexts and cultures.

Johnson and Johnson (2001) argue that more than 40 studies indicate that constructive enquiry produces higher achievement and retention than concurrence-seeking debate. The stages they recommend (and that you may find your supervisors take you through) are:

1   Reaching a position on an issue
2   Being challenged and becoming uncertain about one's views (epistemic curiosity)
3   Actively searching for more information and reconceptualising one's knowledge in an attempt to resolve the uncertainty
4   Reaching a new and refined conclusion.

Defining the argument

In Chapter 4 we looked at some of the traditional arguments in several different disciplines. However, disciplines are on the move, and it is no longer sufficient for a student to be master of one disciplinary approach to thinking. Golde and Walker (2006) describe how students entering doctoral studies in neuroscience can have come from backgrounds in biology, psychology, chemistry or pharmacology (p. 207) and even sociologists are bringing insights to bear on the problems that neuroscientists are involved in. Environmental science is another example of a 'hybrid discipline'; it requires engineering, chemistry, management and psychological understanding. Some music technology courses now demand a high level of competence in physics and computer science, and these are considered as important as any musical background. Appendix C has a list of different terms relating to research methods. It is a useful list to examine if you are working in a cross-disciplinary team and trying to understand what research methods or analytical tools are being talked about or why they people are arguing in different ways.

At the early stages of outlining a thesis Murray (2006) suggests a (relatively) simple exercise that the student can use to structure their argument. She suggests that students use between 25 and 50 words to complete each of the following sentences:

1   My research question is…
2   Researchers who have looked at this subject are…
3   They argue that…

    a.   argues that…
    b.   argues that…

4   Debate centres on…
5   There is still work to be done on…
6   My research is closest to that of X…
7   My contribution will be…

(Murray, 2006, adapted)

Traditionally, critical thinking is considered to be at the heart of doctoral supervision. Browne and Freeman (2000) offer the following definition:

> critical thinking comes in many forms, but all possess a single core feature. They presume that human arguments require evaluation if they are to be worthy of widespread respect. Hence critical thinking focuses on a set of skills and attitudes that enable a listener or reader to apply rational criteria to the reasoning of speakers and writers.
>
> (Browne and Freeman, 2000, p. 301)

Stevenson and Brand (2006) point out that critical thinking is largely a Western, secularist intellectual tradition, and we need to be sensitive to this when applying it in different cultures or to some disciplines. Critical thinking is Western philosophical tradition that encourages analysis, looking for propositions and arguments for and against them. The roots of this approach to supervision are both dialectic and dialogic.

In practice it addresses such questions as 'what is the underlying conceptual framework?', 'what are the arguments for and against?', 'what has been considered and what has been left out?' Wisker (2012) argues that practising using the metalanguage of *viva* defence is a very useful supervisory skill because it ensures that the student addresses gaps in knowledge, boundaries and methodology.

Thinking skills

In this next section we turn to three different ways of examining our own research findings. The first list of coding questions adapted from Donald can be used as a menu to choose from, to identify the most important aspects of your study at any level. The second approach looks at concept maps and the third asks more philosophical questions, which will become important in most doctoral-level work.

Coding key questions for thinking skills

Donald (2002) looked in detail at thinking in several different disciplines (physics, engineering, chemistry, biological sciences, psychology, law, education and English literature), and identified six key components of critical thinking as they applied to each discipline. Table 5.1 has an abstraction of the key components and some illustrations of lines of enquiry that academics might pursue. Donald (2002) gives many further examples for each of the disciplines she has studied.

No student will use all of these thinking processes and behaviours in one piece of research, but they are listed here in Table 5.1 so you can check that you are *consciously* omitting the elements that are not important for you.

Using concept maps to explore links in your data

When we are trying to make sense of how things link together, diagrams are often helpful. We saw a Venn diagram in Figure 5.1 and in Chapter 1 Figures 1.2 to 1.4 were graphical illustrations of different types of doctoral research programme. Concept maps can help you to link together different key ideas and demonstrate impact and sequencing.

Figure 5.2 is a sample concept map designed to explore effective teaching at master's level. The software used is taken from a website that helps people draw their own maps and can be downloaded from that site: http://cmap.ihmc.us/Publications/ResearchPapers/TheoryCmaps/TheoryUnderlyingConceptMaps.htmThere is also further information on concept mapping in work by Kinchin and Hay (2007).

Using methodology (not research methods) to answer the difficult questions

There is an important difference between *research methodology* and *research methods*. Students doing research might be using the same methods but be operating from a very different methodology (or paradigm). So, for example, interviews can be used as a research method by an anthropologist, a phenomenologist, a critical realist and a psychologist, and because of the

Table 5.1 Coding questions that academics might ask to develop critical thinking skills in their postgraduate students

Thinking processes and behaviours		Typical questions the academic might ask
DESCRIPTION		*Describe what you think we are looking at here.*
	Identify context	What are the surroundings in which this is happening?
	State conditions	What elements of this context are essential prerequisites to this happening?
	State facts	What generally accepted information applies here?
	State functions	What normally happens here?
	State assumptions	What assumptions or propositions have been accepted? What do you mean by…? What is your reason for proffering that opinion? But in another situation is the converse true?
	State goal	What is your aim? What are your objectives?
SELECTION		*What were the other options you looked at? Why was this chosen in preference to them?*
	Choose relevant information	What information is particularly relevant to this question?
	Order information in importance	How do you prioritise it?
	Identify critical elements	What are the important units or parts of that information?
	Identify critical relations	Which connections are most important?

REPRESENTATION		*What symbols are relevant here?*
	Recognise organising principles	What laws or rules cover this part of the picture?
	Organise elements and relations	What does a concept map of this area look like?
	Illustrate elements and relations	What are the words or symbols that describe the links between the concepts?
	Modify elements and relations	What connections or concepts can be altered, and how?
INFERENCE		*If x is true, what are the implications? What conclusions can you draw from your findings?*
	Discover new relations between elements	Describe connections between concepts or elements that have not been seen before.
	Discover new relations between relations	Describe connections between these connections.
	Discover equivalence	Is that like anything else?
	Categorise	What classification does that fall into?
	Order	Where in the sequence does it fall?
	Change perspective	What if you were to look at it from another perspective?
	Hypothesise	Does this analysis help you to form a proposition?

(Continued)

Table 5.1 (Cont.)

Thinking processes and behaviours		Typical questions the academic might ask
SYNTHESIS		
	Combine parts to form a whole	Can you see a whole pattern emerging?
	Elaborate	Describe that pattern in more detail.
	Generate missing links	Where are the gaps? What do they not explain?
	Develop a course of action	How can we prove, expand, and/or illuminate this phenomena?
VERIFICATION		***How can we test the validity of this finding? What examples can you give? What evidence can you show?***
	Compare alternative outcomes	Is there any consistency across different contexts, over different times?
	Compare outcome to standard	How does this result compare to what might be expected?
	Judge validity	What is the soundness of these results? In how many ways could we prove it wrong? Would we get the same result if we used different experimental methods?
	Use feedback	What feedback are we getting? How do we need to adjust to it?
	Confirm results	What test–retest or triangulation strategies do we need to employ? Are the findings repeatable?

Source: Adapted from Donald (2002, pp. 26–27)

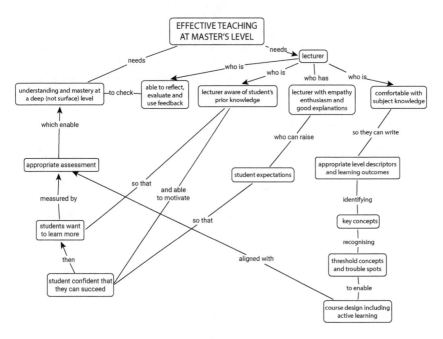

Figure 5.2 A Sample concept map: effective teaching at master's level

different philosophical backgrounds of each, they will draw different conclusions.

Understanding your methodological perspective is a doctoral-level requirement and will enable you to answer questions such as:

- How do you choose your sample or the texts you examine? How do you bound an archive? How do you choose a canon?
- How did X get published, funded and become influential?
- Is there a reasoned argument here?
- What is the generalisability of your work?
- How do you situate your methodological approach within an epistemological framework?

If you want to explore different methodological approaches further, Quinn Patton (1990) has some helpful definitions.

Understanding and articulating the methodological perspective you have embraced will enable you to identify any assumptions you might have unwittingly embraced. This is particularly important when it is easy to generate lots of data, but questioning where it came from and what it implies is not always so evident.

Collecting all your thoughts together

Some researchers find it very helpful to have a whiteboard or a large piece of paper on a wall where they can collect key pieces of information as they emerge and group ideas together. Sticky notes are ideal for this task because they are provisional and can easily be rewritten and refined as your thoughts progress. This process can make writing up much easier. The sorts of headings that you might include are:

- **Area of concern/problem**
    - o   In this section you collect ideas that describe the field you are inter-ested in.

- **Assumptions/paradigm/philosophical position**
    - o   Here you are looking to identify issues that you are not including as well as any methodological position you are taking.

- **Ethical issues raised**
    - o   An important section where you will collect ideas relating to research procedures and wider issues.

- **Literature/references/key contributors to the field**
    - o   A summary of the findings of your literature search, including summarising any limitations that you have identified in existing literature.

- **Hypothesis/research questions**
    - o   Sometimes clearly articulated from the beginning in experimental sci-ence but emerge and evolve in other disciplines.

- **Sample/context**
    - o   Purposive, random etc.?

- **Research methods**
    - o   Research methods considered; those chosen and those discarded.

- **Theories/findings**
    - o   In this section you are getting close to some conclusions.

- **Impact/stakeholders/gatekeepers**
    - o   Identifying why this research might be important, for whom, ques-tions for further research.

These issues can all be marked up on a canvas, whiteboard or spare wall, and used as a sorting place for ideas (see Figure 5.3).

Area of concern/problem	Assumptions/paradigm/philosophical position	Ethical issues raised
Key references/authors	Hypothesis/research questions	
Sample	Research methods	Theories/findings/contribution to the field
Stakeholders/gatekeepers	Impact	

Figure 5.3 Sample noticeboard design: collecting it all together (amended and adapted from the Research Design Canvas; original available from www.academic-toolkit.com/researchdesigncanvas)

If you have the opportunity to present this as a 'work in progress' in a collaborative forum, perhaps with other research students, you might like to use a digital tool to gather ideas from the group. Padlet is one useful tool (currently free) for doing that: https://en-gb.padlet.com/

Solving problems in a logical manner – applied research projects

Problem solving is part of critical thinking, but it also has elements of action implied within it and is therefore important for applied projects. It can be linked to project planning in terms of skills, and requires some critical thinking skills, planning skills and some people management skills.

Swartz and Perkins (1990) describe a typical problem-solving procedure which I have adapted here to include elements of implementation suggested by Coverdale (Taylor, 1979; see Figure 5.3). There are three key stages: description, investigation and implementation. The descriptive stage can call upon similar critical thinking skills to those introduced by Donald (above), but Swartz and Perkins add in specifically an evaluation of working in an uncertain world. This leads to the need for a risk assessment of each option eventually identified (which is part of the dialectical procedure).

This problem-solving procedure also introduces the concepts of key values. Ethical issues were discussed briefly in Chapter 3, but it is obvious that they cannot and should not be kept out of the picture when we are considering critical thinking.

The investigation stage should provide much of the information needed for the implementation stage. For example, if the necessary resources come as a surprise in the final phase, it means that the investigation was not carried out thoroughly.

For the planning and implementation stage there are a variety of project planning tools available, as we saw in Chapter 3. Figure 5.4 summarises the links between the functional and critical thinking approaches, as applied to project planning. A version of this simple staged approach can be used by students at all levels to help them design a research project.

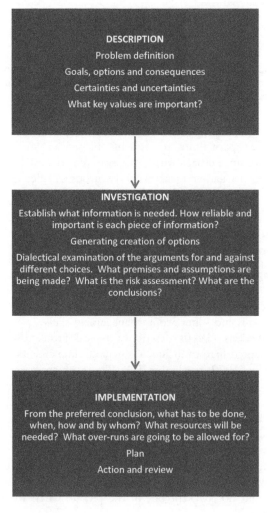

Figure 5.4 A problem-solving procedure

Reflecting metacognitively on performance

Metacognition refers to observing, reflecting and directing our thinking. The question is: 'how do we learn how to do this?' The ability to reflect at a high level is not only required by those undertaking social science degrees. Researchers from the hard pure subject groups spoke of the need for students to learn from mistakes and how coming to terms with failure could make them better scientists in the long run. We look at how to deal with this type of situation more in the next chapter on emancipation.

Definitions of reflection

The term 'reflective thinking' was used by John Dewey (1933) to describe the thinking process people use when faced with questions of controversy or doubt for which their current understanding or solution, for whatever reason, is no longer satisfactory. According to Dewey, a 'reflective judgement' is the end goal of good thinking: the judgement or solution that brings closure to the problem (if only temporarily).

The definition of reflective learning provided by Boud, Keogh and Walker (1985, p. 19) states that reflection is about providing intellectual and affective activities for learners to explore their experiences 'in order to lead to new understandings and appreciations'.

Reflecting metacognitively will help you to answer three important questions about your research:

1   What is the impact of your own subjectivity on this work?
2   What cultural frameworks have you espoused?
3   How has this changed as your research has progressed?

A comprehensive overview of reflection as an aid to learning was carried out by Moon (2000), which largely built upon and evaluated the work of Schon (1991) and Brookfield (1995). Schon looks at the reflective practitioner as someone who remains open to discovery and seeks that discovery by reviewing and reflecting on their actions. As Moon also points out, Schon's famous distinction between reflection-in-action and reflection-on-action may not always be clear-cut and in his original work he discusses whether reflection in action is possible for the artist, or whether deconstruction ruins the art form.

Brookfield (1995) argues strongly for reflection when he asks teachers to 'build in some element of self-evaluation whereby students can show you that they are learning, even if to you their progress seems non-existent' (p. 180).

There is growing belief that solidifying the reflective part of Kolb's experiential learning cycle aids student learning. The original learning cycle had four separate stages which suggested that (1) learning took place when action and

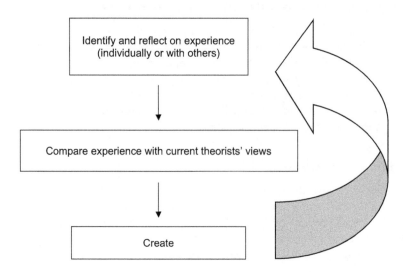

Figure 5.5 A model of reflection

experimentation became (2) conscious experience which the individual used to (3) reframe their understanding of what was happening; this act of reframing led to (4) generalisation and the creation of theory (Cowan, 2008).

Another dynamic model of reflection adopted is represented by the flow chart which also becomes a continuous loop (Figure 5.5).

The importance of discussing your work with other researchers

By engagement in peer discussion and linking it to scholarly literature, we can monitor our developing experience. This provides alternative perspectives that support critical reflection.

The conceptual underpinning of this model of reflection is rooted in constructivism, the learning theory which also underpins research and argues that you cannot simply give others your understanding of an area – we have to constructively engage to build our own understanding. Moreover, social constructivism argues that in building complex understandings, an essential role can be played by peer collaboration to promote reflective development. This links to Schon's (1991) notion of the reflective practitioner and to the identification of two sorts of professional reflection – reflection-on-action that occurs after the event, and reflection-in-action: 'the idea that professionals engage in reflective conversations with practical situations, where they constantly frame and reframe a problem as they work on it, testing out their interpretations and solutions' (Calderhead & Gates, 1993, p. 1).

Cowan takes the Kolbian model one stage further when he expands on Schon's distinction between reflection-in action and reflection-on action. He argues that there is also reflection-for action, and that in between each stage different reflecting skills are required.

This well-known model of reflection in action, on action and for action can help us to identify three sets of questions that prompt these different types of reflection (see Figure 5.6).

Moon reminds us that the ability to reflect may depend upon maturity (thus introducing the whole person into this generally more depersonalised approach). She gives examples of students' work and approves of those that:

- show evidence of an internal dialogue and self-questioning
- take into account the views and motives of others and consider these against their own
- recognise how prior experience, thoughts (their own and others) can interact with the production of their own behaviour

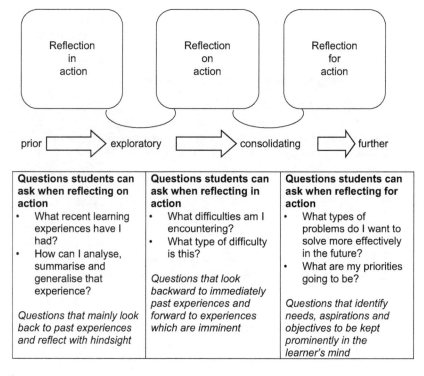

Questions students can ask when reflecting on action	Questions students can ask when reflecting in action	Questions students can ask when reflecting for action
• What recent learning experiences have I had? • How can I analyse, summarise and generalise that experience? *Questions that mainly look back to past experiences and reflect with hindsight*	• What difficulties am I encountering? • What type of difficulty is this? *Questions that look backward to immediately past experiences and forward to experiences which are imminent*	• What types of problems do I want to solve more effectively in the future? • What are my priorities going to be? *Questions that identify needs, aspirations and objectives to be kept prominently in the learner's mind*

Figure 5.6 Questions to support reflection in, on and for action

Source: After Cowan, 2008, p. 53

- show clear evidence of standing back from the event
- show that the students helps themselves to learn by splitting off the reflective process from the points they want to learn (e.g. by an asterisk system)
- show recognition that the personal frame of reference can change according to the emotional state in which it is written, the acquisition of new information, the review of ideas and the effect of time passing.

(Moon, 2004, p. 209)

There is a balance that needs to be struck between the need for guidance against the desirability of students doing their own thinking without too much help. How much help to give must be influenced by level of study and prior experience, together with the goals of the course.

Becoming a reflective professional is about including some of these processes in our daily lives. Moon also recommends keeping a reflective diary as a way of capturing incidents and focusing our attention on our own professional development. Increasingly, requirements for continuing professional development (CPD) are asking for evidence of reflection and subsequent professional growth. Some students using qualitative research techniques will already be keeping such a diary and will need to incorporate evidence from it in their final thesis. Box 5.1 summarises a range of questions that you can address through writing a research diary. They will help you develop your metacognitive skills.

Box 5.1 Helping to develop metacognitive skills

Do you keep a research diary to:

1   Show evidence of an internal dialogue and self-questioning, especially questioning why you are doing this research now
2   Seek to understand the views and motives of others and consider these against your own

3   Recognise how prior experience (both yours and that of others) can affect your research
4   Demonstrate that you can stand back from the event
5   Identify your learning points and then examine **how** you learned them?

Recognise that the personal frame of reference can change according to the emotional state in which it is written, the acquisition of new information, the review of ideas and the effect of feedback.

This chapter ends with two quotations from supervisors which demonstrate the centrality of critical thinking to working with postgraduate students:

An outstanding student, is someone (who) really has a lot of get up and go and is I think an average student is someone who just really needs a lot of help to try and question ... What we teach fundamentally in graduate school is how to solve a problem, research methods and theoretical tools and methods and how to take a problem and solve it or address it in a convincing way we teach them how to do things, how to answer questions.

What we don't really teach people in a systematic way is how to recognise the questions and to frame them in tractable ways. That's really the difference between a good and an average student. They all have the methods, research methods and skills and the literature and you know have ... the ambitions for writing a thesis, for example, but the really good students are the ones that can go that next step and actually can formulate interesting problems. Those are the ones that really stand out because those are the ones that are going to really advance the field. The ones that have sensitivity in respect to a question ... that is something that you don't teach in any courses. It's like my seminars, that's what I talk to students about. OK that is what I praise them for when they do, that when I feel like I have to give them a lot of affirmation for, when they take that step, because that's really the unusual part, the part where I kind of stand up and applaud.

The stages of development that were first identified by Perry (1970) have spawned profound research about how we can move our beliefs about knowledge (epistemological development) and embrace an ontological perspective (become and embody whatever philosophical position we decide to espouse). This element of how critical thinking can lead to transformation is further explored in the next chapter on emancipation.

Questions for further contemplation

How does knowledge appear in my subject?

How does knowledge appear to me?

What questions should I be asking of my data?

In this chapter we have explored a range of approaches to critical thinking, both from the purely analytical perspective and aspects such as reflection and metacognition, which also enable an increase in personal awareness. It is these aspects that can be particularly difficult to entangle if trying to allocate interventions to either the critical thinking or emancipatory approaches. The dividing line is whether the intent of the intervention is personal growth and autonomy or the purer development of just a cognitive ability. In the next chapter we consider emancipatory interventions in more detail.

Chapter 6

Finding your own way

Enabling emancipation

The emancipatory approach: an introduction

Students who value this approach to doing their research say that finding their own direction is important to them. The student working from this approach would want support and challenge, but not necessarily direction about how to do a project (that level of direction would come from an enculturation approach). Although failure usually hurts, learning from failure is one of the things we embrace when working from this approach. We recognise it as an opportunity to learn from experience.

We can immediately see that if a supervisor is working from an enculturation approach and the student wants freedom and emancipation, there can be a clash. The same can be true the other way around – the supervisor wants the student to make their own decisions, to become an independent researcher, and the student feels unready for this and seeks more guidance about how to do things appropriately.

Creating an emancipatory environment through using enquiry-based learning

At an undergraduate level, enquiry-based learning (EBL) is a common first step towards doing research. The supervisor is initially a guide, and gradually later becomes a collaborator. This whole approach is intended to encourage you to become actively involved in designing the questions, researching and constructing knowledge. It is a process of learning which includes (but is more than) using research and study skills. Ideally it is holistic (and not limited to cognition) and offers opportunities for creativity. Because it is so different from a didactic approach to teaching, it requires different learning outcomes and assessment strategies; it is often a useful part of the process to engage a whole group of students in co-designing the assessment criteria. It is often used to work with transdiscipline/multi-discipline issues of constructed knowledge (including addressing the theory–practice gap), ethical dimensions, and the interface of human/technical working.

While enquiry-based learning (EBL) it is not a new approach to teaching and learning, it has recently been newly emphasised in universities. Its purpose is to develop transferable skills of enquiry to enable coping with complexity and enquiry-based learning is now a recognised strand in academic practice. In the UK it attracted £4.5m of government money to fund a new centre for excellence in teaching and learning (CETL) at Manchester University and several other CETLs were introduced with similar themes.

Tosey led an enquiry-based learning project at the University of Surrey which investigated how those who said they were using enquiry-based learning methods actually worked in practice. He argued that there are five key dimensions to EBL. One of those dimensions involved the head, the heart and the hands. His definition is that

> EBL is a process of learning in which the learner has significant influence on or choice about the aim, scope, or topic of their learning. This process of learning draws upon research skills and study skills, but enquiry is not reducible to either research or study.
>
> (Tosey & McDonnell, 2006, p. 2)

Hutchings (2007) has described the differences between the traditional teacher and the tutor who focuses on enquiry-based learning in the following way. He argued that the traditional teacher provides materials, sets the boundaries and teaches in a tutor-centred manner. In contrast, the EBL tutor will facilitate learning by establishing target learning outcomes and providing triggers for learning *while the students* collectively examine the problem, decide on the areas requiring more research, conduct the research, collate the information and re-examine their learning.

The shift required at a doctoral level is that everything is operating at a more sophisticated level and then moves one stage further. The supervisor will want to move from being guide, to facilitator, to collaborator and then (because a doctoral student will have created new knowledge) to learn from the researcher.

The root of the word facilitator comes from the latin *facilis* which means 'capable of being done'. It is thus something that is capable of being done, and therefore the facilitator's role is to create the conditions under which a task may be effectively carried out. It is the opposite of to define, to limit or to close down (Gregory 2006).

This is an approach to designing learning activities which is part of a suite of active learning approaches, but it is less directive than problem-based learning where students work on solving a problem pre-defined by the teacher. One way of looking at different types of active learning is portrayed in Figure 6.1.

The three terms – problem-based learning, enquiry-based learning and action learning – are widely used, and frequently muddled up. It is worth spending a little time disaggregating them so you can understand more

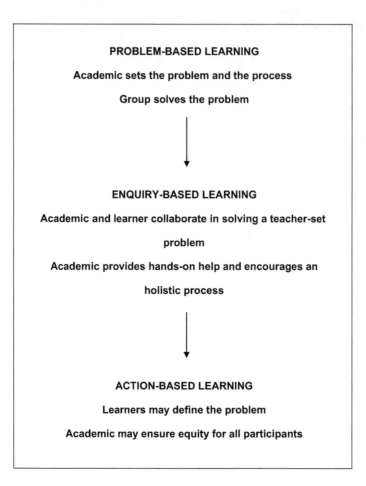

Figure 6.1 Different approaches to active learning

clearly what your supervisor might be expecting of you in different situations (bearing in mind also that they might be operating from slightly different definitions). The three terms are all members of the same family in that they involve the student in active learning. But they are different in the amount of control that the supervisor exerts over the agenda. In this sense I believe that problem-based learning and action learning are polar opposites.

In problem-based learning the academic will set the students the problem. For example, students will be asked to 'mend, and if possible improve this toaster' rather than be told in a transmission-based manner that 'today we are going to study the flow of electricity through metals'. True problem-based learning will encourage exploratory research. It will encourage students to apply a variety of interpretative contexts in order to allow them to develop their own sense of which is appropriate and it will encourage an active and creative engagement of the students with the creative potential of the subject (Hutchings, 2007).

In action learning participants take ownership of formulating the problem. Beaty describes action learning as 'a continuous process of learning and reflection, supported by colleagues with an intention of getting things done. Through action learning individuals learn with and from each other by working on real problems and reflecting on their own experiences' (2003, p. 4). A common method of the facilitator 'controlling' the action learning group is to ensure that each participant has the same amount of time to present their story (Weinstein, 1999, p. 157).

Enquiry-based learning moves the academic away from their role as being the fount of all knowledge to becoming a knowledgeable equal. In reality, between enculturation and emancipation there is an overlap and blurring which is described in Figure 6.2. For the purposes of analysis we are looking at them as separate approaches.

The questions for students to explore are: what type of learning is my supervisor trying to organise? How can I get the best from this particular situation?

Finding a supportive environment

Habermas argues that emancipatory knowledge means that social constraints must be made apparent and a supportive environment is required. He proposed that there is 'a basic human interest in rational autonomy and freedom which issues in a demand for the intellectual and material conditions in which non-alienated communication and interaction can occur' (Carr & Kemmis, 1986, pp. 135–136).

As we have seen in Chapter 4, a supportive environment can come from many sources. Table 6.1 is one for you to amend and then fill in. If you want to be in charge of your research, then you need to identify a wide range of sources of support and advice, especially at doctoral level.

Working with an emancipatory supervisor

The emancipatory supervisor will be acting as a non-directive mentor who offers challenge and support but who is not seeking to guide their student in any overall direction apart from that of personal growth. Emancipation here has a very different objective to enculturation – typically the academic who is working within an emancipatory framework is not necessarily seeking to keep their student focusing on a career within their discipline.

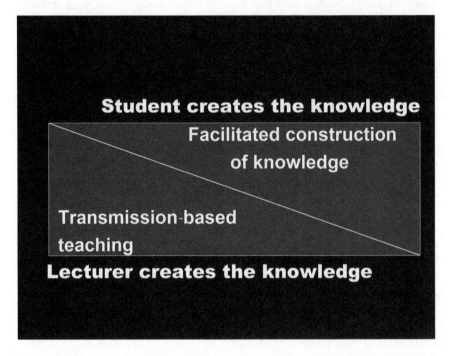

Figure 6.2 The overlap between transmission-based teaching and facilitated construction of knowledge

The emancipatory supervisor is not the absent supervisor. While in the past that was a common form of supervision in some cultures and at some universities, it is not considered satisfactory today. Discussing expectations about how often you might meet and what feedback you need is part of the next chapter.

Defining personal development planning

One way of looking at personal development can be through the lens of creating independent learners, citizenship and employability. In the UK, personal development in higher education is now considered in the context of the Dearing Report (1997), where it was argued that all university graduates at all levels should have access to personal development planning (PDP). What PDP should consist of was not clearly defined.

While the QAA have defined personal development planning in higher education in the UK, there is no universally or internationally recognised definition of what PDP really is (Brennan & Shah, 2003). In the UK universities were

Table 6.1 Empowering the doctoral candidate doing research: what do you need to know – where can you go?

Please use these headings as suggestions to stimulate the creation of your own

	Supervisor 1	Supervisor 2	Grad school adminis-trator	Post-docs	Peers/ previous candidates	Grad school	Specialist librarians	IT/web/ handbooks	Student support services/ medical	Family/ friends	Other
Induction – finding your way around, meeting key figures											
Key departmental meetings to attend											
Understanding standard of work expected											
Managing formal paperwork and procedures											
Clarifying the research question											
Literature to read											
Creating a supportive intel-lectual group											
Mediating											
Technical support											

(Continued)

Table 6.1 (Cont).

Access to data											
Experimental design											
Seminar/conference participation											
Analysis of results											
Discussing department's policy on authorship and co-authorship											
Creating a supportive peer group											
Feedback on written work											
Creating a network											
Job opportunities/careers advice											
Viva preparation, organising a mock viva											
Emotional support											

Appeals procedures									
Friendship									
Financial advice									
Housing advice									
Health and nutrition									

asked to develop progress files: *'a means by which students can monitor, build and reflect upon their personal development'* (Dearing, 1997).

The UK's national Quality Assurance Agency (QAA) guidelines state that PDP is concerned with learning in a holistic sense (both academic and non-academic) and a *'process that involves self-reflection, the creation of a personal record, planning and monitoring progress towards the achievement of personal objectives'* (QAA, 2001).

The guidelines also give statements about the intended purpose of PDP, i.e. to enable students to become more effective, independent and confident self-directed learners, to understand how they are learning, to relate their learning to a wider context and to improve their general skills for study and career management.

In Australia, at the University of Sydney, research has been carried out on graduate attributes. They have included: scholarship, lifelong learning and global citizenship as desired attributes (see Barrie, 2004, 2006, and the University of Sydney Graduate Attributes Project). More recently in Australia, attention has focused on enabling research students to identify, articulate and develop the skills and attributes that they already have. This enabling approach is particularly appropriate for experienced, mature students but it demands of the research supervisor the ability to encourage the research student to consider and reflect on the processes they are participating in (Cumming & Kiley, 2009).

In a research-led university in the UK personal development planning was defined as falling into three slightly different separate subgroups:

1   Learning, research and scholarship
2   Employability and engagement with society
3   Personal and communication skills.

Each level of academic study had different learning objectives and course and module leaders had to be able to demonstrate that their students were achieving at least one objective in each sub-group (Burden & Lee, 2006).

Part of personal development planning is understanding what transferable skills you are developing through your research and where any gaps might be.

Employability: how important are transferable skills?

Through Salzburg I and II (EUA, 2010) the European Higher Education Area has set the direction of doctoral education as an international process of researcher development and knowledge generation that requires quality assurance, encourages mobility, and enables dissemination and the development of transferable skills.

The European Universities Association (EUA) has pointed to several important new challenges for doctoral education in the future: the risk that the pressure to publish might compromise research integrity, the digital challenge requiring new technical, legal and ethical attitudes, and the fact that research is increasingly international and global which challenges, among other things, the mobility of our researchers (EUA, 2017). All of these add to the existing requirement for research education to provide the link between knowledge generation and knowledge implementation. It is at this point that transferable skills become most important. An international education can enable intercultural competence and ethical challenges can introduce new ways of looking at the ownership of knowledge.

Earlier in Chapter 1 we explored the EHEA Framework for Higher Education. This, too, emphasises the importance of developing communication skills, teamwork and a positive attitude towards continuous learning.

What transferable skills might students doing research develop?

One way of analysing this is to look across the framework of five approaches. Table 6.2 shows some of the generic skills that will be useful in almost any walk of life, and which can come from undertaking a significant research project.

The skills shown in Table 6.2 above will be useful for demonstrating competence in almost any interview situation. So the most important thing is to identify examples which substantiate your claim to having a skill and be able to turn it from your example to a generic claim and then to a hypothetical example in your next employer or interviewer's world.

The language around transferable skills for researchers has been codified most comprehensively by Vitae, a UK-based body that has published the Researcher Development Framework (RDF). It posits that there are four domains for development (knowledge and intellectual abilities, personal effectiveness, research governance and organisation, engagement, influence and impact; see www.vitae.ac.uk/researchers-professional-development/about-the-vitae-researcher-development-framework/developing-the-vitae-researcher-development-framework).

Recognising the transferable skills that are being developed

Vitae.ac.uk have created a commercially available online planner for assessing transferable skills and undertook a great deal of work in identifying transferable skills at doctoral level. Many of these can be usefully applied at other curriculum levels as well. In Figure 6.3 the RDF is reproduced in full. Some universities link their transferable/generic skills training closely to the descriptors used by Vitae.

The inner circle refers to the four domains covering the knowledge, behaviours and attributes of researchers. It sets out the wide-ranging knowledge,

Table 6.2 Generic and transferable skills that can arise from doing a research project

Functional	Enculturation	Critical thinking	Emancipation	Relationship development
Project planning skills	Assimilates professional expertise	Makes a logical and persuasive argument	Able to move into new environments	Considered trustworthy
Project management	Becomes a valued team member	Anticipates flaws in assumptions and logic	Skilled in communicating to different groups of people	Clear values
Time management	Communicates persuasively with colleagues	Has forecasting skills and knows the limits of forecasting	Can make decisions and choose a route forward	Emotionally intelligent
Negotiates for necessary resources	Understands and can work with different cultural imperatives and values	Problem solving	Assesses own strengths and weaknesses	Cares for others
Monitors progress			Learns from difficulties. Plans to enhance knowledge and skills	Respects and manages personal and professional boundaries

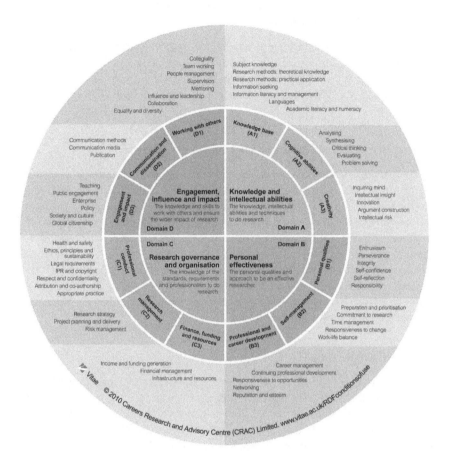

Figure 6.3 The Researcher Development Framework

Source: www.vitae.ac.uk/researchers-professional-development/about-the-vitae-researcher-development-framework/vitae-researcher-development-framework-rdf-full-contenthi-res.jpg

intellectual abilities, techniques and professional standards expected to be able to do research, as well as the personal qualities, knowledge and skills to work with others and ensure the wider impact of research. Within each of the domains there are three sub-domains and associated descriptors.

The framework was derived from semi-structured interviews with researchers, literature reviews, reports, sector-wide consultations and expert panel review. Its aim is to identify attributes in a non-judgemental, inclusive and forward-looking manner (Reeves, Denicolo, Metcalfe & Roberts, 2012).

Five approaches to using the Researcher Development Framework in practice

The RDF was designed to be available for higher education institutions in the UK. Many other universities have access to tools on its website. It is possible to use the five approaches to research supervision to suggest different ways of using the RDF within a supervision setting. Table 6.3 makes some suggestions.

Being a member of a small research group

Much academic research is carried out in small groups, so learning to contribute positively and gain from being in these groups is an important skill. Many groups start by agreeing their ground rules around confidentiality and participation. Although it may sound pedantic, agreeing at the beginning that no one member is going to be allowed to dominate or talk over everyone else is a useful way of averting future trouble. Some supervisors are very skilled at managing the group dynamics and for others it is more challenging. Do not hesitate to ask for help if you feel your group is becoming dysfunctional. If your supervisor has not handled this particular type of problem before, they should be able to find someone who can.

Finding a mentor

Mentoring is a powerful concept for the student seeking emancipation (Pearson & Brew, 2002). There is much literature on mentoring in general and facilitation skills in particular (Lee, 2006, 2007). The mentor is usually seen as a non-judgemental adviser. Mentoring builds upon Rogers' belief that self-experience and self-discovery are important facets of learning (Morton-Cooper & Palmer, 2000) and it involves acknowledging that adults can move from being dependent to being self-directed, accumulate experiences and create a biography from which they can learn and change. The expected movement is from needing to acquire knowledge and being subject centred to becoming more performance centred. The objective is the application of experience and the development of sound critical thinking abilities.

A mentor can be primary or secondary (Kram, 1985; Freeman, 1998). The secondary mentor has much more of a business-like relationship with their mentee. They concentrate on providing support for career development. They can suggest projects, help to solve work-based problems, provide coaching where they have particular skills and might actively promote their mentee where they think it could be helpful.

The primary mentor can provide a more profound experience and some academics will feel that this goes beyond what they are expected to do. When an emotional bond is developed the mentee is deemed to have a primary mentor

Table 6.3 Five approaches to using the RDF in practice

Functional	Enculturation	Critical thinking	Emancipation	Relationship development
Establish what courses and tools the careers service provides	Use tools from the RDF website to get the research group or members of your department to plan how to enhance each other's potential	Examine the principles behind the RDF (see Reeves et al., 2012) and decide whether or not they help career planning and interview skills. Are there alternative approaches to identifying transferable or key attributes that would be more useful?	Encourage the researcher to review all the different lenses to identify where their strengths might be well placed and what areas they might need to develop. The different lenses include: engineering, information literacy, leadership, public engagement, teaching and researcher mobility	Share own experiences of developing an academic career and link them to the RDF. Explore what has changed and what might change in the future
Get the researcher to read relevant parts of the Vitae.ac.uk website and follow up any relevant courses that the RDF might indicate	Read experienced researchers' profiles. Is there anything helpful to role model?			

and the approach to supervision is moving towards the next category in the framework – building a relationship of friendship. The strength of the primary mentor is that they provide acceptance and confirmation that the mentee is worthwhile and this leads to personal empowerment. They can help the mentee to learn from a variety of life experiences as well as planning and rehearsing future encounters.

Secondary mentors are obviously easier to find. Sometimes a relationship starts with more functional, secondary mentoring expectations, and goes on to become extremely fundamental for both parties.

Emancipation as a process implies that you will receive both support and challenge. It is also a process which allows and supports personal transformation; the potential for the research process to be transformative becomes clear when we look at the prerequisites for transformative learning: it is perceived as requiring critical reflection and a disorienting dilemma (Mezirow, 1991; Taylor, 2007).

This element of enabling you to cope, while also giving you information which may disturb and disorientate you, can be challenging for all academics. Some may believe that this period of disorientation needs to be deeply experienced if you are to understand a phenomenon; others may feel that this is cruel and unnecessary and the dilemma can usually be resolved through discussion about the place of disorientation in higher education. If this is a problem for you as a student doing research, you may need to seek further advice from a trusted member of the academic community or student support services.

Learning through failure

There is a fine role for failure. As Bandura (1994) noted, if we experience only easy successes we have no opportunity to develop resilience and emerge stronger through adversity. This extract from an interview below demonstrates this point in practice.

> I had a student working on a project that I considered very, very good and she was somebody who... was probably better at analysis of data than collecting data and she kept collecting data that just didn't make sense ... to us. It was becoming clear that she was not a great person in the lab, so I thought, oh well ... maybe she is not that good an experimentalist, you know, we will have to teach her how to do things. But it wasn't that at all, it was just there was something there, in her data that we were just completely missing. We really had to have thought totally, totally differently and we missed it so I feel guilty about missing it because a group in (another major university), in fact, didn't miss it ... and as soon as they reported their findings we understood ... exactly why ... it wasn't working and, you know, she spent nearly two years doing that ... And this frustrated her to no end, she was really unhappy and bitter about it. And yet I think it made her a much stronger scientist, and then she started doing

things, other things ok ... we just started doing things that worked more easily and she got her degree ... she was there for six years, I think, two years of her experience was unpleasant, because she wasn't getting things to work. She came with two of her peers, and came the same year who were just getting everything to work. So she was bound to feel why are things not working? ... But in the long run, you know, I don't feel that badly, although I recognise and I do feel it myself, the frustrations are something we all have to go through. You know, we have to learn how to deal with this kind of frustration, because she is going to face it again. If she takes a path in her career in science. And, I ... fully expect her to appreciate that in the long run even though she didn't, she doesn't now.

A good mentor or supervisor will know how to help a student learn from difficult experiences and from failure. Clutterbuck and Ragins argue that the quality of the relationship is more important than whether the relationship is formal or informal (2002, p. 45). This observation demonstrates yet another blurring of the boundaries, in this case between the emancipatory and relationship approaches.

Mentoring also has its dark side. The uncritical mentee faced with an untrained mentor who is burdened with a lack of self-awareness can be a problem. Berglass (2002) has shown how some coaches 'gain a Svengali-like hold over both the executives they train and the CEOs they report to' (p. 91). Darling (1985) coined the term 'toxic mentors' and these include avoiders, destroyers and criticisers who would take unfair advantage of their mentees. Egoists could be added to the list. This begins to explain another necessity for training in supervision: academics need to be particularly aware of the dangers of mentoring over issues that they have not fully resolved themselves. The boundaries need to be clearly thought through. The mentoring academic does not direct, they 'midwife' the project, dissertation or thesis and it can take some time to understand this position and to develop the skills to perform it.

The limits of the role of mentoring for the research student

A mentor can be an appropriate significant other who can provide honest guidance, support and challenge at the right moments for their mentee. Thus the true mentor does not have to be a 'supervisor', and should not be a line manager or an assessor. (Various organisations and professions have appropriated the term 'mentor' and applied it in these ways.) The quality of a pure mentoring relationship is one which is voluntarily entered into and where there is already a positive regard on both sides. It can provide a profound learning experience (for both sides). The research supervisor can take a mentoring approach, but because of their organisational role and obligations they may have to manage the conflict of interest that is inherent in adopting this approach.

When is mentoring most beneficial?

Critical incidents can provide rich food for reflection, but often past experiences can be used as a gateway to reveal more about present concerns. The experienced mentor will spot such opportunities to open doors and reveal trends or illuminate blind spots (Egan, 2002). Mentoring is used to help mentees into a new role or organisation, to fast-track their development, to develop cross-cultural awareness, to aid coping with managing change, to help manage the conflict between the professional role, patient autonomy and organisational demands, to help manage the cloak of defence against emotion and to help those who are seeking explanations of their own perceived inadequacy (Morton-Cooper & Palmer, 2000). However, it is worth emphasising that mentoring is for the well, not for the sick.

Separating

The mentoring relationship usually ends at some point, often because the period of study is completed but sometimes there is a problem with the ending. An unaware mentor can 'cling on' and the mentee can experience a sensation of wanting to escape and reclaim their life. Regular reviews are necessary in advance to establish when the formal mentoring relationship will close. A friendship or working relationship might then continue, but it would be different. It is easier to mark the separation by meeting in a different place, or agreeing to do something different at a final session.

A mentoring relationship is inherently a professional one. In this chapter we have looked at many aspects of doing research from an emancipatory perspective. We have covered different approaches to enquiry-based learning, empowering yourself, identifying transferable skills, working in small research groups and finding a mentor. In the next chapter we explore the other side of this line, where the relationship between academic and student becomes more personal and altruistic, energising and rewarding for both parties, yet still stays within appropriate boundaries.

Chapter 7

Creating and maintaining relationships

The relationship approach: an introduction

In this approach academic and student will seek to have a friendly relationship, to anticipate and normally avert unnecessary conflict. Problems will be solved with good will, and overt rationalisation will not always need to be expressed for either party to do what is requested. Appropriate boundaries will be observed. Many supervisors prefer to work within a professional relationship and not to be seen to be offering friendship. Students, however, may be seeking more nurturing and resolving this tension is an important part of managing this approach. There is some evidence to suggest that candidates value this fifth approach, *relationship development*, more than their advisors do (Löfström & Pyhältö, 2015).

The quality of a relationship between teacher and student has been recognised as an important, even the most important, determinant of student satisfaction with teachers (Harkin, 1998; Smith, 1997; Carson, 1996). Poor relationships have been linked to poor completion rates (Taylor, Kiley & Humphrey, 2018) so in this context we are seeking what Clarkson (1995) called a 'working alliance', a productive alliance around a shared task.

Friendship is an important and controversial part of this approach, but it is challenging in the context of education. Aristotle argued that friendship is essential – 'nobody would choose to live without friends, even if he had all the other good things' (see Thomson, 2004, p. 258). He divides friendships into those of utility (which the other four aspects of the framework in this book could fall largely into), erotic friendships (which cross a boundary of acceptability in working with and assessing students) and perfect friendships.

Perfect friendships are based on goodness and are obviously the most valuable; here friends care more about the other person than they care about themselves. Moreover it means liking the other person for what he/she is, not for any incidental quality that they might possess such as beauty. Such friends have similar attributes and such friendships only occur after a long while. The relationship needs time to develop. According to Aristotle you cannot get to know each other until you have eaten the proverbial quantity of salt together. This apparently is a *medimnos* or one and a half bushels. In other words, the friends need to share many meals together, mealtimes traditionally being times of social chatting, anecdote-telling and story swapping. Finally there are few truly good friendships for there are few truly good people.

(Vardy & Grosch, 1999, pp. 32–33)

Macfarlane (2009) introduces Aristotle's moral virtues into this arena when he calls for (among others) courage, temperance, liberality, magnificence, friendliness and wittiness. He points out that the twin pressures on academics of the massification of higher education and the pressures to research combine to put virtue and ethics under greater strain. If we are to develop a holistic approach to supervising the student who does research, the existence of this pressure explains why it is so important to explore this final strand of the framework: developing the relationship

A good relationship does not necessarily imply that friendship was experienced at the beginning of the research process. Ives and Rowley (2005) suggested that friendship can get in the way of a good supervisory relationship because it might blunt the ability to be critical. 'The power dynamic between supervisor and student makes friendship difficult' (Ives & Rowley, 2005, p. 536).

Wisker and colleagues (Wisker, Robinson, Trafford, Creighton & Warnes, 2003a; Wisker et al., 2003b) argue that emotional intelligence and flexibility play a large part in working with students through to successful completion. Emotional intelligence has become a contested but popular phenomenon in this field. It has been usefully demonstrated that there are four main aspects to emotional intelligence: perceiving and expressing emotion; understanding emotion; using emotion to facilitate thought; and managing emotion in self and others (Salovey & Mayer, 1997). Some academics will be naturally more interested in and able to notice emotion in their students than others. One student spoke for many when he said:

> The more pastoral support of the supervisors was really important. I remember being surprised at how helpful they were. This was as important in helping me to get through as any intellectual support.

Part of managing emotion is the ability to manage conflict (Salovey & Mayer, 1997). One supervisor was asked how they tried to resolve conflict.

> Well, I just try to rationalise things and, you know, try to see to what extent I can take away the emotions and bring, you know, usually by talking to the students, very occasionally by talking to the adviser. In really, really bad cases I've taken on a student who did not get along with his or her adviser.

The literature of coaching and organisational development can help us to understand more here. Morgan (1997, pp. 205–209) suggests that there are five different ways of handling conflict (based on a study of chief executives): avoidance, compromise, competition, accommodation and collaboration. As Harrison (2002) points out, each situation requires an approach appropriate to the situation.

> Sometimes collaboration will not work; it may be better to go for compromise through negotiation in order to preserve all players' commitment and to move the game forward. Sometimes it may be wise to abandon a chosen course in the interests of making progress on another front.
>
> (Harrison, 2002, p. 121)

The relationship between the academic and the postgraduate student can be a very close one. Consequently, much time is spent debating how we identify appropriate boundaries. It is very difficult working with a student who is seriously hurting, for example being bereaved, hungry or ill. Normally your supervisor's role here would be to point you to professional sources of help.

Contracts are useful, whether they are formal or a discussion of expectations. Students need to raise the idea of having a working agreement sensitively. Many supervisors now pre-empt this discussion and that makes it easier for you. An agreement or contract frees us to act within the terms of a contract without needing to check whether or not we are working within expectations all the time. However, (psychological) implied contracts need to be made as explicit as possible for several reasons. First, the clarification of expectations means that both parties are likely to work together harmoniously for longer and unexpected violations are less likely to happen. Second, when changes happen, the impact on the contract can be fully prepared for.

Contracts take into account the differences in power between the parties. In the student–supervisor relationship the academic has power over resources, knowledge and expertise; the ultimate power lies in the assessment procedure; and there is some residual power in giving references. The student has some power over the academic's need to meet completion targets and other aspects of the academic's reputation. This cannot (yet) be a relationship of equals. Hockey (1996) recommends that explicit contracts should be agreed between student and supervisor, and argues that this is a much-neglected approach.

The healthy relationship requires more than a bald analysis of power over resources. It requires agreement over boundaries. In negotiating the boundary over confidentiality Hawkins recommends a discussion about promising and expecting limited confidentiality.

> In negotiating the appropriate confidentiality boundary for any form of supervision, it is inappropriate to say everything is confidential that is shared here, or that nothing here is confidential ... we also give our

supervisees the undertaking that we will treat everything they share with us in a professional manner and not gossip about their situation.

(Hawkins, 2006, p. 209)

Creating a healthy relationship: the importance of trust

Central to a healthy relationship between student and academic is the issue of trust and a belief in each other's integrity. These are elements which are both reputational and revealed over time. Both the student doing research and their academic supervisor will have reputations to be created and developed, and these are nurtured through a positive regard for each other. In practice, this means that a healthy relationship is developed when each keeps their promises. This is true both of the little things (for example, arriving at meetings on time and prepared) and the bigger things (for example, following up on a discussion about putting in a joint grant proposal, belief in the accuracy of results).

Trust as a workplace phenomenon has been defined as 'willingness to accept uncertainty and make oneself vulnerable in the face of insecurity' (Hope-Hailey et al., 2012 in Guccione, 2018, p. 4). Guccione examined the opportunities for trust to form within in the doctoral experience. Both supervisors and students described a range of experienced vulnerabilities. For students, vulnerabilities were related to the intense learning (both explicit and tacit) involved in the doctorate and academic environment, and the challenges of shifting prior learning strategies to doctoral study. For supervisors, issues were related to structural issues in how supervision is viewed, valued, supported and constrained by departmental and institutional policies and cultures.

Guccione (2018) also asked how trust in doctoral supervision relationships is built or broken. Both supervisors and students entered into new partnerships with an implicit or assumed trust in each other, based on prior educational attainment or institutional affiliation. Trust on both sides was built over time, both in response to each prior encounter and to observations of behaviour or attitudes towards others. Trust erosion also occurred gradually over time and was linked to unfulfilled expectations for the supervision relationship, or mismatched ideas about the purpose and process of a doctorate. Acute incidents related to deception, bullying or personal integrity issues caused trust to be broken in a way that forcefully damaged the relationship. Hawkins (2006) recommends that breaches in trust are not seen as irremediable, but as opportunities for reflection, learning and relationship building (p. 210).

The framework highlights the movement from (and between) professional and personal identity (see Table 2.1). This creates a potential conflict because academic goals can conflict with personal goals.

Managing expectations is key to creating a longer-lasting relationship (Kiley, 2006; Murray, 2006), and it is important to explore these expectations. Murray identifies a dichotomy in expectations over writing a thesis and explores what happens when students want to learn how to write more concisely and use correct terminology, whereas supervisors' concerns were reported to be about the nature of and evidence for a solid argument.

One experienced supervisor described how they set expectations:

> I always say to them you can go through a love–hate relationship with me. It will probably be more hate than love most of the time, but if we can come out of it at the end still talking to each other, possibly even friends or colleagues in the future, that for me is a good outcome.

The power of first impressions cannot be ignored in establishing expectations. The first encounter with an academic and the induction of new students is central to creating a good working relationship. The aim is to establish a working alliance where, at the contracting stage, expectations are shared along with hopes and fears.

Learning as a member of a group from the beginning

The first few weeks are crucial for understanding and establishing expectations. This can be helped by joining, creating and working with a group early on. A typical introductory programme for a management school is shown in Box 7.1 and a similar programme (which would include more on research methods) might be designed for doctoral students. Some universities have established Graduate Schools, and introductory programmes can be organised under their auspices.

Box 7.1 Outline induction programme for master's students

Introduction to the institution and key academic and administrative staff
Introduction to working at master's level:
    The skills of critical analysis
    Referencing for writing journal articles, theses and dissertations
    How to get and use feedback
What can you expect from teaching methods at master's level:
    The role of lectures, case studies, tutorials etc.
    Identifying how you learn best and managing time
    An outline of new technologies to be used
Introductory case studies in small groups
Feedback from group work
Experienced postgraduate students form a panel to respond to questions from new students
Social event

Creating or joining a cohort group

The induction process is a key time for you to make your own alliances, to find fellow students who are starting their research at the same time as you, so that you can create your own less formal support groups. At this stage, although it might seem important that you are working with people who are studying the same topic as you, in fact what seems to be even more important is that you have started at the same time. Creating a cohort group that agrees to meet regularly, where you can take turns to describe how you are getting on, is one of the most positive things you can do to aid your successful completion on time.

Groups of doctoral students are also created by joining a doctoral school, doctoral college or centre for doctoral training. These groups can act as a buffer against the danger of isolation. If you are not already part of an existing network it could be important to start forming your own.

Assessing your induction as an individually recruited postgraduate student

It is just as important (and easier to forget because the relative informality of the situation means that we can be tempted to make assumptions) that individually recruited research students will need a thorough induction as well. Below is a checklist for assessing your own induction (Box 7.2).

Box 7.2 Assessing your induction as a postgraduate student

Checklist for inducting postgraduate student(s)

1. **Establishing expectations**
   Have you discussed what your supervisor expects from you and what you are seeking from your supervisor?
   Have you resolved any differences?

2. **Setting study targets**
   Have you identified the main milestones in your individual study plan?
   Have you agreed an overall timetable?

3. **Keeping records and referencing**
   Have you started to summarise, record and correctly reference your work?
   Do you know where to go to get advice on avoiding plagiarism?

4. **Enhancing their library skills**
   Have you met the subject librarian?
   Have you undertaken a library induction?

5. **The student as part of an academic team**
   Have you met other students and members of your academic and administrative team?
   Have they got a list of names, job titles and telephone numbers of key people in the department?
   Do you know where the common room facilities are?

6. **Aiming early for academic writing at postgraduate level**
   Have you offered early pieces of writing and asked for feedback?
   Have you found excellent examples of writing in your discipline?

7. **How do you overcome isolation?**
   Have you met others from your home region and/or from your discipline and formed a cohort group?
   Have your found the postgraduate facilities?
   Are you involved in appropriate conferences?

8. **How do you help to frame a research proposal?**
   Have you discussed with your supervisor why you want to do this particular research?
   Is it practical and at the right academic level?
   Is it too close to your emotional world?

9. **Who is the main tutor/supervisor?**
   Have you discussed your availability?
   Have co-supervisors discussed with you how they have allocated different roles between themselves?

10. **Where can you get help in managing your finances?**
    Do you know sources of help?

Seeking and using feedback

Research students will need to learn to cope with sporadic, sometimes extensive and sometimes difficult feedback so an early discussion about this can be very helpful. Feedback asking you to revise the way you are looking at something does not mean you have failed – it means you are being given opportunities to learn. It can be useful to seek feedback from a range of sources (post-doctoral researchers, other academics and postgraduate and other students), so that supervision sessions are more likely to include healthy debate and be more interesting.

The second discussion to have about feedback is much more practical: a discussion about what you can expect feedback on (short assignments, essay outlines, draft articles or whole chapters of a thesis?) and how much time you should expect to elapse before it is given. Do you prefer to get feedback in writing or face to face?

The student as part of an academic team

In many universities doctoral students are treated in a similar way to junior academic members of staff, and this is a good way to be included as a member of the academic tribe. In Norway and the Netherlands, as we have seen before, doctoral candidates are recognised as full members of staff and have a salary. They tend to have slightly longer contracts if they are also expected to teach. Master's students and undergraduates may or may not have quite such close access to academics, but as we have seen, they do need to be encouraged to create their own learning communities. Some departments or teams already have learning groups, and give them some occasional form by suggesting they discuss certain books or journal articles, or invite certain speakers.

Overcoming isolation

Isolation, and the fear of isolation, challenges most of us (Grenyer, 2002; Hockey, 1994). A research student who is a member of a minority ethnic group, living and working for the first time in a new country where the cultural expectations clash with those of the homeland can feel exceptionally lonely. However, domestic students can be isolated, too; they can find the environment foreign and be unwilling to challenge an academic intellectually or to ask for help socially. A key for many students' ability to complete their studies is whether or not they find friends and colleagues with whom they can work and socialise. You can use the sample outline induction programme (Box 7.1) to help the formation of these groups. Time spent on the formation of study groups early on in the induction procedure can make all the difference to you being able to maintain momentum during the whole of your studies. While the induction period is a golden opportunity for encouraging the formation of study groups, it is not the only one. Box 7.3 summarises a list of suggestions that can be implemented at any time.

Box 7.3 Overcoming isolation

Have you:

1   Encouraged small peer groups of students to form and meet regularly
2   Attended and got involved in departmental research seminars
3   Invited other researchers to present their work

4   Considered starting a journal club
5   Got involved in wider activities
6   Worked out how to explain your research project in an interesting way to friends and/or family who have had no connection with your study?

Establishing your own professional network

It is not uncommon for students to be muddled about where to turn for different kinds of help. You may have personal tutors, advisors, academic tutors, primary or co-supervisors, contract researchers, course directors, programme directors and lecturers.

At doctoral level it is possible for candidates to be confused about the role of the primary supervisor. For example, is their role to be the focal point of contact with the student, or is it to mentor the second supervisor? Some of this confusion may be deliberately allowed to continue because an academic is embarrassed to admit that they are themselves being mentored – and therefore might be seen by their student as inexperienced. At other times the primary supervisor might have taken notional responsibility for a large number of students, and not been able to focus on the needs of every individual. In the previous chapter, Table 6.1 presented a matrix of topics and people that you can adapt to include local issues and sources. The intention of this type of matrix is that it will foster and enable you to handle independently some of the issues that will arise while you are doing research.

How do you get help with managing finances?

University students are adults and academic staff are not *in loco parentis*. However, if a doctoral student is being funded as part of a team through a research council or other grant, the university has an obligation to ensure that the student does receive that agreed amount of funding over the required time-span. Up to one-third of students in the UK do not expect to complete within the minimum three years (Kulej & Park, 2008), and this pattern is repeated across Europe (EUA, 2007). This is why time management is so important. It is crucial that you have planned how to pay fees, living and travel expenses and any research costs, even if you have been offered a fully funded place. Some students plan to do their writing up while they are working – and some achieve it. However, I am an advocate of writing up as much as you can while the research is in process because it usually makes the final task easier.

Most UK universities have student hardship funds, some departments have access to (often strictly limited) funds to support doctoral students and there are some charitable trusts that will help – but all of these take time and planning, so the student who suddenly finds their finances have run out may be in trouble.

A common source of supplementary funding for postgraduate students is to undertake marking and teaching. This is considered useful preparation for an academic career and can be a positive addition to a CV, but the pay levels for this type of work vary considerably. Supervisors will be keen to ensure that a reasonable balance between paid employment and research time is maintained.

The most predictable source of funding is usually when employers sponsor students who are also their employees. Norway is an example of a European country that regards doctoral students as employees anyway, and supports them as members of staff. Students taking professional or practitioner doctorates may also be supported by employers and there usually is a trade-off between autonomy over the research project and funding. Box 7.4 has some questions you may want to consider before starting your research project.

Box 7.4 Questions to ask to help students planning and managing finance

Planning to manage your finances

1   Is funding assured (or realistically will it be available) for fees and living expenses for the minimum time of study?

2   Have you costed travel, books, software, communication tools and stationery?

3   If you have a part-time role or salaried post as well, how much time are you expected to work for?

4   What charitable/student union/hardship funds might be available? What are their criteria for allocating funds and how long does it take to get access to them?

5   What is the difference between full-time and part-time fees? How easy is it to move between them?

6   What will you do if your research runs over time?

7   Are any penalties incurred if you fail to complete?

Researching emotive subjects

There are some functional constraints that bear on the choice of topics to research. I am discussing this issue here because although there are functional answers to some of these dilemmas, they can be experienced as relationship strain if there is something you want to do and you feel you are not getting support from your supervisor.

Some students have a deeply held personal motivation to study a topic, and hope to find a resolution for a personal dilemma. In other cases it is a means to an end – often a job. There are some students who want to undertake personally risky fieldwork – this can mean travelling to countries where there are unstable political regimes or health risks, and some students want to study issues that they are trying to resolve for themselves, for example anorexia, bereavement or sex. There are also students who may want to study techniques or pursue experiments where the academic has some ethical concerns about the long-term application of the findings. In all these cases, where there are practical, emotional and/or ethical dilemmas, you have some extremely difficult decisions to make.

You may have a proposal which should really be a fully funded research programme, where the risks that you are going to take need to be carefully evaluated and planned for, your supervisor has health and safety obligations and the university has a duty of care. Insurance and ethical approval may be an issue. In some of these cases you may need to divide your research project into phases: phase one is linked more to acquiring the necessary research skills and phase two (the research project you really want to undertake) takes place after graduation, and can even become a life's work.

If a supervisor has serious ethical concerns about the nature of the research proposal (an extreme concern could be, for example, that the results of the research are going to be used for coercion), then they have the right to withdraw. Your supervisor has an obligation to support you undertaking a realistic, ethically sound project where they feel competent to support you. You have the right to have a professional relationship with a supervisor where previously agreed expectations and boundaries are maintained. Withdrawal by a supervisor or an application by a student for a new supervisor is disruptive, but sometimes the best solution when everything else has been tried. It should take place with the advice of senior members of the department and with good will.

Can you identify degenerate patterns in relationships?

There are at least four potential abuses of the supervisor–research student relationship, and they can work both ways. A supervisor can abuse the relationship with a student and vice versa.

One party may be seeking *commercial gain* from the other's research. This could be direct financial reward for claiming a part in an invention that was not their due, publishing work where there is no previous co-authorship agreement, or putting in funding bids excluding the other and overemphasising their role in the work carried out so far. One party might be seeking *intellectual gain*, where they seek to enhance their own reputation from claiming authorship where they

Table 7.1 Establishing a good relationship from the beginning

Establishing a good relationship from the beginning Supervisor and student can complete separately and then discuss	1	2	3	4	5	
DESIGN						
1 It is the supervisors' responsibility to select the research topic						It is the student's responsibility to choose the research topic
2 The supervisor decides the appropriate theoretical framework						The student decides which theoretical framework or methodology they should use
OWNERSHIP OF KNOWLEDGE						
3 Supervisors need to have detailed knowledge of the research topic						Supervisors need a general knowledge of the research topic
4 The supervisor is the specialist						The student is the specialist
5 The supervisor is an authority figure						The supervisor is a colleague, acting as a sounding board
6 Supervisors should go with students to academic conferences						Students should attend academic conferences independently
7 The supervisor is responsible for ethics and the standard of the final thesis						The student is responsible for ethics and the standard of the final thesis
TIMING						
8 The supervisor should have a timetable in mind and ensure the student keeps to it						The student should create their own timetable for their research and monitor their own progress
9 Supervisors should arrange the appropriate number of meetings						Students should ask for meetings when they need them
10 The supervisor should initiate a discussion about the timing for submitting the final thesis						The student should initiate a discussion about the timing for submitting the final thesis
11 Students should always adhere to agreed deadlines						Agreed deadlines are guidelines rather than absolute targets

(Continued)

Table 7.1 (Cont.)

Establishing a good relationship from the beginning Supervisor and student can complete separately and then discuss		1	2	3	4	5	
WRITING AND FEEDBACK							
12	Supervisors should correct style, grammar and spelling as well as content						Supervisors should only correct content, not grammar and spelling
13	Supervisors should encourage students to publish in academic journals before their thesis is submitted						Writing academic articles before submission takes too much time
14	Supervisors should make explicit how often they are willing to give written and/or oral feedback						Supervisors should give as much feedback as the student needs
15	The supervisor should assist in the writing of the thesis if the student has difficulties						The supervisor advises only, and leaves all decisions concerning content, format and style to the student
16	The supervisor should insist on reviewing drafts of every section of the thesis						It is up to the student to ask the supervisor to review drafts of the thesis
17	Students need fully honest feedback, even when it is very critical						Supervisors need to judge how much feedback to give

Source: Adapted from various versions. See Kiley, M. & Cadman, K. (1997) *Supervision expectations*. Adapted from work by Brown, G. & Atkins, M. (1988) *Effective teaching in higher education*, pp. 146–147. London: Methuen.

have contributed little, or they can be too controlling. There are problems associated with seeking *sexual gain*, but the final problem area is much more difficult to put a satisfactory boundary around. *Friendship gain* can be legitimate, but where it is an abuse of power or feeding a need to be loved it can become oppressive. In these (hopefully rare) instances it might be important to seek support from a harassment advisor, union representative or counsellor.

It is easy to talk about establishing boundaries, but it is much more difficult to do. Sometimes external help from a counsellor needs to be sought, and if this is done in time it can make all the difference to the experience for all parties concerned. There are ethical issues to be addressed about conflicts of interest if a supervisor is seeking gain and these are compounded when the academic has a role in assessment. In these difficult cases a discussion with the programme manager or director of postgraduate studies will be needed.

The best relationships arise where values and expectations are shared, where trust is high, feedback is kindly but honest, where problems become opportunities to learn and all parties are respected for their contribution.

How to have a healthy relationship: understand and manage expectations from the beginning

The best way of establishing a healthy relationship is for all parties to explain their expectations in a non-confrontational manner. Table 7.1 is intended to be used between students and supervisors as a discussion document. It can be adapted to stimulate discussion with groups, and different elements might be emphasised for different stages during the research programme.

In this chapter we have explored various elements that are important for creating a healthy relationship between supervisor and the student doing research. Table 7.1 is probably the most important document in this book. In the next chapter we combine the framework and apply it in practice to many different situations to demonstrate how strength comes from blending all these approaches.

Chapter 8

Using the framework to help your research

Which approaches are best?

This is a common question and there is only one answer to it: no one approach is 'best'. It is in the understanding of different strengths and needs, and in blending them, that they become really useful. Using Macfarlane's (2009) analysis of the functional approaches to undertaking research, in Table 8.1 we look at how using the other approaches can enhance the work that needs to be done to complete a sound research project.

To demonstrate how negative it could be to focus on only one of the five approaches, look at the advantages and disadvantages of each. Or rather, look at the disadvantages, which become more apparent if that approach is pursued exclusively. Table 8.2 explores this point.

Toxic mentoring (a disadvantage of emancipation) refers to when the mentor has not resolved issues from their own previous experience that surface again within the mentor–mentee relationship. It can also be part of degenerate relationships, which we discussed in Chapter 7.

Working towards independence

One way of recognising a good researcher is that when they have completed their research project they have become an independent researcher (this is often applied at master's and doctoral levels). On further analysis dependence and independence mean slightly different things within each approach, so to achieve independence you might seek mastery of as much as possible of the following. Table 8.3 explores this further.

Encouraging creativity

At this stage I want to look at how the framework can be used to explore one of the core elements of research: creativity. At levels 6–8 (UK National Framework) or the EHEA description of the 'first to third cycles' (bachelor's to PhD level) it is apparent that there is international agreement that being creative is a key activity for all research students: at the bachelor's level this falls within the requirement to be able to solve problems in complex and unpredictable

Table 8.1 Carrying out a research project using all the different approaches

Functional phases of managing research	Enculturation	Critical thinking	Emancipation	Relationship development
Framing	Looking at other examples in the discipline	Asking: what is excluded? What is assumed? Completing a risk analysis	Assessing where this approach could take the student both professionally in their career and personally	Discussing whether this is something that 'we can work on together'
Negotiating	Asking who else in the department or discipline is doing similar work What opportunities for collaboration might there be? What contacts might be approached?	Looking at collaboration and links to work in or across other disciplines	Who else in society might be usefully included or involved in this work?	Discussions about the tenor of the approaches to be made and how to negotiate effectively
Generating	By reviewing the research methods most commonly used in the discipline. Looking for opportunities for joint fieldwork	By identifying and arguing for the most appropriate research methods Creating new research methods	By exploring and understanding the methodological imperatives behind different approaches to research and the implications of these approaches	By sharing own research methods, experiences and concerns

Creating	Through team discussion. By analysing data, looking for advances in the field	By creating new models and theories and critiquing their generalisability	By linking advances to areas of personal growth	By sharing the interpretative process
Disseminating	Through departmental seminars and conferences	Through conference discussions, responding to referees' reports, writing journal publications and books. Further grant applications. On how knowledge is created/discovered	Through performance and open discussions Wider publications (not necessarily just academic journals)	Shared publications and presentations
Reflecting	On epistemological progress On how the team supported and were involved in the research process	On the appropriateness or otherwise of the implicit and explicit frameworks employed	On impact on self and ontological development	On impact on relationship development and ability to work productively Also assessing the impact on friends and family

Table 8.2 Advantages and disadvantages of different conceptual approaches to teaching and supervising research students

	Functional	Enculturation	Critical thinking	Emancipation	Relationship development
Advantages	Clarity Consistency Progress can be monitored	Encourages standards, participation, identity, community formation	Rational enquiry, fallacy exposed	Personal growth, ability to cope with change	Lifelong working partnerships Enhanced self-esteem
Disadvantages	Rigidity when confronted with the creation of original knowledge	Low tolerance of internal difference, sexist, ethnicised regulation (Cousin & Deepwell, 2005)	Denial of creativity, can belittle or depersonalise student	Toxic mentoring (Darling, 1985) where tutor abuses power	Potential for harassment, abandonment or rejection

Table 8.3 Moving towards independence as a researcher

| | PROFESSIONAL ROLE → | | | | PERSONAL SELF |
	Functional	Enculturation	Critical thinking	Emancipation	Relationship development
Dependence	Student needs explanation of stages to be followed and direction through them	Student needs to be shown what to do	Student learns the questions to ask, the frameworks to apply	Student seeks affirmation of self-worth	Student seeks approval
Independence	Student can programme own work, follow own timetables competently	Student can follow discipline's epistemological demands independently	Student can critique own work	Student autonomous. Can decide how to be, where to go, what to do, where to find information	Student demonstrates appropriate reciprocity and has power to withdraw

circumstances; at the master's level students are required to demonstrate originality in their application of knowledge and at the doctoral level there is
a requirement to create original knowledge (QAA, 2008; EHEA, 2018).

Creativity is also a personal construct and is one of the areas where there
needs to be understanding created between supervisor and student. How does
your supervisor understand creativity? One supervisor said the following, but
there are many other interpretations of this concept; 'For me, creativity is
when we walk between two worlds, the metaphysical and the physical.'

Kleiman has drawn a phenomenological map of creativity in learning and
teaching (2008, p. 211) and Hargreaves (2008), coming from a nursing background, argues that we need to encourage creativity, but identifies a tension
between creativity and managing risk.

Sternberg and Lubart (1995) argue that creativity requires various intelli-
gences (synthetic, analytic and practical) and a mixture of psychological, intellectual and environmental opportunities. They write about how important
a level of knowledge is if we are to be able to discern what is truly creative and
original, and they explore other issues such as motivation, thinking skills, persistence and an optimum environment.

Originality is going to be judged first by those within the discipline, so there
is an enculturation element in the types of challenges we set.

> I gave her a problem I honestly thought would form a very large part of her
> PhD it was so challenging. And she came back literally the next day and said
> she'd thought of a solution and would I like to see it. And she had done it!

In this case the supervisor went on to explain what the challenge was in
supervising such an able student.

> I think it was close to brilliant I would say. It was incredibly inspired. And
> she went on to do some very significant things. I would say she was so
> bright than even in papers she was publishing some of the reviewers strug-
> gled to understand the subtleties of what she was saying. In her particular
> case my main focus was how to develop her communication skills and how
> to present material, because there was no question she was right, it was
> just a question that other people often had difficulty understanding where
> she was coming from with it.

Creativity and originality is a crucial test of a good piece of research. It is quite
possible for creativity to be encouraged by any of the approaches to study (see
Table 8.4). This could be seen as moving along the suggested dimensions of creativity as a constraint-focused experience to a fulfilment-processed experience
(Kleiman, 2008, p. 212). Table 8.4 below represents only the beginning of an
important debate

In Table 8.4 perhaps one of the more surprising elements to emerge is that the
functional approach can also encourage creativity. An example of this arose in an

Table 8.4 Approaches to doing research and encouraging creativity

Creativity as constraint focused ————————→ Creativity as fulfilment focused

	Functional	Enculturation	Critical thinking	Emancipation	Relationship development
Creativity might arise from:	A reaction or resistance to constraints	A process of incremental change	Purposeful exploitation of chance occurrences	Reaction to disorientation	Creating something new that has personal value

interview with a supervisor from outside the scientific paradigm (which is significant because in laboratories it is common for teams to work long hours), who said:

> I think they find the direction difficult, that I have been so directive. I think they thought that they could swan in and wander around the literature for a bit and do what they liked ... so I have insisted that they are here 9am– 5pm five days a week. That is very hard for them ... I am beginning to think the structure helps to make creativity, I would never have believed I would have said that. I think it is because people know where the boundaries are, they know what they have got to achieve and this helps in achieving that ... they are putting up (creative ideas) on the wall ... there is a sense of freedom in the structure I think.

Many are used to juxtaposing the concepts of emancipation and creativity, but the reaction to constraints and criticism can also force the formation of new ideas. Table 8.4 uses Kleiman's work to illustrate how different approaches to supervision might encourage creativity.

Analysing further the difficult questions that can arise for students during a research project

In Chapter 2 a list of 30 possible questions from students doing research was introduced and an initial suggestion for finding some solutions was made (Table 2.3). Here we explore how using the five approaches might increase the range of options for answering some of those difficult questions.

These statements have been taken from comments made by students in difficulty. No one student will face all these difficulties, but using the framework as a problem-solving tool can help us to find a combination of answers that should help.

All these solutions can look 'neat' when packaged in a table in a book, and they will not apply directly to you. However, if you are faced with an apparently intractable problem and think to yourself 'in how many ways could I approach this?' the work of this chapter will be done and the chances of a successful outcome for everyone will be greater.

There are two key questions that I have been asked, to which (for once) there are simple answers.

Q1:   What, in your experience, is the most important approach?
A: It is the *flexibility* to adapt and combine that is most important
Q2:   Are there any common characteristics of poor use of these approaches?
A: *Inflexibility*

This framework has been shown as a matrix for the purposes of deconstruction and analysis. A more realistic map of the doctoral process is shown in Figure 2.1 where you can see that functionality is all surrounding. A researcher–supervisor relationship cannot exist outside an institutional context, but the centre is

Table 8.5 Using the framework to find answers to some common questions

Question	Functional	Enculturation	Critical thinking	Emancipation	Relationship development
How do I manage time when I have a busy part-time job and no sense of direction for my research? I don't know how to manage my time, it seems always to be chasing me.	Find some time management books/courses	Focus on research direction first. What are your options?	What are the criteria for choosing between the options, e.g. is it career, an interesting topic that will keep you motivated or the chance of working with an excellent team?	What do you really want to do?	Who can give you good advice on this?
My project needs more funding but my supervisor seems to think I can manage without any more resources. What can I do?	Write a realistic and costed project plan. Present it to your supervisor and be prepared to negotiate	How does this fit into the department's work? Is there room for gaining from collaboration?	Explore all options in detail, cost alternatives	Do you need to go elsewhere or can you get sufficient from this situation to achieve your objectives?	Who can I turn to for advice about how to handle this?

(Continued)

Table 8.5 (Cont).

Question	Functional	Enculturation	Critical thinking	Emancipation	Relationship development
I complained about the lack of meetings and was told emails also count as supervision	Have a discussion about how much time is available for supervision and plan meetings/contact for a year ahead bearing that in mind	Are there others in the department/ research team you can also get feedback from? Peers, post-docs?	Review what is considered reasonable with others to check you have formed a reasoned judgement	Assess whether this is a tenable situation for you	Explore expect-ations (see Table 7.5)
I don't know if I can do this	Set yourself shorter deadlines. Focus on the next immediate goal not the whole project	Discuss with your peer group/cohort group to get sup-portSeek expert assistance if the problem is technical	List everything that is troubling you. Are there any common threads emerging?	Have you had this feeling before? How did you overcome it then?	Get some reassur-ance about the level of support available. This statement may need considerable investigation
How much teaching should I do? Can I do? Can I say 'no'?	Review time manage-ment and assertiveness skills	Discuss with your supervisor, seek a mentor or course where you can get help with preparing teaching efficiently	What are the advantages and disadvantages of undertaking more work?	Assess how important this is to your well-being	Are there others in a similar position?

redolent of the heart that this framework carefully puts back at the centre. Emancipation and enculturation are seen more in opposition and are connected by the other three approaches.

This framework is intended to be just a starting prompt for problem solving. In this chapter we have seen that every approach has advantages and disadvantages, and that every approach can be used to support your journey towards becoming an independent researcher. In the next chapter we will look at ways of using the framework to help you write as an academic would.

Glossaries to help further inquiry

The terms in these glossaries (Box 8.1) are allocated to the five different approaches so that if the reader wants to study a particular approach further, there are signposts available. In practice, however, the application of these terms is not confined to just one approach.

Box 8.1 Key terms to help further enquiry

Key terms mostly related to the functional approach

Advisor: academic advisors act as personal and/or academic tutors and as supervisors to postgraduate students' research projects in some countries. In the USA a research supervisor is called an Advisor.

Credits: a credit measures both the quantity and quality of learning and in the UK equates to 120 hours. Level 7 is typical of the learning expected at master's level and level 8 is typical of the learning expected at doctoral level.

Marking criteria: a set of criteria that are applied to assessed work. They can be defined in a series of subcategories, e.g. literature search; knowledge and content; compliance with instructions; synthesis; conceptualisation; conclusions; communication and presentation; referencing.

Master's degree: a course of postgraduate study typically made up from 180 credits of which xx have to be at level 7 and the rest can be at level 6 (see QAA.ac.uk). The master's programme can be a taught programme or achieved by research (MPhil).

Module: some universities offer courses made up from modules, or blocks of learning, measured by credits. A module will involve learning at one particular level.

Module leader: the academic who is in charge of planning the teaching and assessment for the module, and who will oversee students' progress through that particular part of the course.

PhD (Doctor of Philosophy): a programme of research at doctoral level.

Postgraduate certificate: typically 60 credits at master's level.

Postgraduate diploma: typically 180 credits at master's level.

Programme accreditation: a programme can be made up from a series of modules and will have a number of credits. Each university will have an accreditation procedure to check that the programme will be taught at the required level and the students and staff will have the necessary resources.

Practitioner doctorate: a programme of study at doctoral level which includes taught courses and research in an applied field. It includes the following qualifications – Doctor of Business Administration (DBA), Doctor of Clinical Practice (DClinPrac), Doctor of Education (EdD), Doctor of engineering (EngD) and Doctor of Psychology (PsychD).

Professional doctorate: doctorates that focus on embedding research in a reflective manner into another professional practice. These are the same as practitioner doctorates.

Supervisor: the academic who is responsible for ensuring that the university fulfils its responsibilities to the student.

Key terms in ethical thinking

Codes of practice: these are produced by professional bodies to give guidelines for good practice and to create a rule book for identifying unethical behaviour. They are related to duty ethics because they are ultimately imposed. They arise out of normative ethical approaches.

Deontological ethics: argues that ethical meaning is found in principles such as the 'Ten Commandments' or the Kantian imperative to 'treat equals equally and unequals unequally', which can apply in all situations. An action is right or wrong, independent of the consequences, and the end does not justify the means (Gregory, 2006a).

Discourse ethics: ethical meaning emerges from discourse enabling reflection on values and the discovery of shared norms. Getting the discourse right would therefore be of the highest priority (see Habermas, 1992).

Duty ethics: not a true ethical stance; a person who does their duty because they feel obliged to, that they ought to, is not necessarily acting morally.

Global ethics: builds on the sense of connectedness stressed by the feminist ethics; it stresses responsibility for the environment and human kind globally.

Normative ethics: takes on the more practical task of arriving at moral standards that regulate right and wrong conduct. This may involve articulating the good habits that we should acquire, the duties that we should follow, or the consequences of our behaviour on others.

Teleological ethics: in contrast to deontological ethics, utilitarianism argues that the end does justify the means. Utilitarianism is a consequential theory. The utility (hedonic) calculus suggests calculations about the right decision can be made on the basis of: intensity, duration, certainty, extent, remoteness, richness and purity.

Virtue ethics: looks at a person's character. It asks, 'what sort of person should I be?' Commonly held values are the Rogerian attributes of 'integrity', 'respect for others' and 'empathy'. The Aristotelian attributes include: truthfulness, modesty, temperance (balance and moderation), rightful indignation, courage and justice.

Key terms mostly related to enculturation

Apprenticeship: an opportunity to learn by practical experience, working with skilled and experienced people in their trade, art, or calling.

Coaching: instructing and directing intensively.

Communities of practice: a group of people with a common purpose – joining this group requires a process of socialisation.

Enculturation: the process of socialisation into the discipline, the working milieu (e.g. the academic department and the university) and the national culture. A person is 'enculturated' when they are comfortable being or working at all these levels; they have learned the traditional content of a culture and assimilated its practices and values. Their membership of the relevant groups is accepted and others may seek their advice on such matters. It usually requires a long period of study and an ability to acquire tacit knowledge.

Epistemology: the theory or philosophy of knowledge. In the context of this book it particularly applies to the epistemology of different disciplines and will include an understanding of boundaries, presuppositions and an agreement about what is to count as valid knowledge.

International student: any student who is studying in a culture that is not native to them, and who may be unused to the food, language and predominant religious or cultural practices.

Legitimate peripheral participation: the first stage of inviting a newcomer to become a member of a community. It is a low-risk invitation which usually has a social element to it (e.g. attending conferences); it is about learning *to* talk with other members of the community. There is an element of apprenticeship and socialisation, before being able to become a full participant in the community.

Ontology: a branch of metaphysics concerned with the nature of being, the study of the essence of things. In the context of this book it refers particularly to someone who instinctively reacts as a member of a disciplinary community. They have become a member of the discipline (as opposed to merely having an epistemological understanding of it).

Tacit knowledge: hidden knowledge which is not easily articulated but which is a powerful contributor to how people think and act. It is transmitted socially through being a member of a community. New members of any community need to be aware of tacit knowledge to be able to participate effectively. This is not propositional or scientific knowledge.

Key terms mostly related to critical thinking

Concept maps: a diagrammatic depiction of a set of concepts and the relationships between them.

Deductive reasoning: reasoning from a general statement or definition to a particular instance.

Dialectical thinking: elements considered in relation to each other. A dialogical discussion (see below) where reasoners put one (or more) argument(s) in competition with each other. A court hearing or a debate are examples of dialectical thinking.

Dialogical thinking: a discussion (or dialogue) about an issue from different perspectives or frames of reference.

Epistemology: the philosophical study of theories of knowledge.

Inductive reasoning: reasoning from a particular instance or fact to a general conclusion

Knowledge: the act of having a clear perception or understanding. It is based on understanding and skill, which are, in turn, based on thought, study and experience. Knowledge cannot be divorced from thinking minds. It is produced, analysed, evaluated, maintained and transformed by thought. A book contains knowledge only in the derivative sense – it only exists because minds can access it. Knowledge is not to be confused with recall.

Metacognition: awareness of the thought processes being used.

Proposition: a larger unit of analysis than a concept, defined as a statement that expresses relationships among concepts and that has a truth value.

Socratic questioning: a deeply probing technique intended to uncover meaning, truth, understanding or beliefs.

Syllogism: a deductive inference consisting of two (or more) premises which are assumed to be true, and a conclusion. A syllogism can create a misleading impression as in the following example: *Cows eat grass; grass is eaten by cows; so all grass is eaten by cows.*

Key terms mostly related to emancipation

Authenticity: coming out or being open about one's feelings. When the academic owns his or her feelings, they are said to be 'congruent'.

Emancipation: to be freed or liberated from oppression.

Empathy: sensing the student's private world (e.g. fear, confusion, elation) as if it were your own.

Mentor: a trusted key person to help reflection. The mentor can help by encouraging questioning of the governing variable(s), support the mentee in their journey from the known into uncharted territory, and focus on learning opportunities.

Mentoring: an emancipatory act. Although the term 'mentor' has been appropriated in some professions to include notions of assessment, the pure conception of mentoring is to encourage personal growth.

Personal Development Planning: a conscious process of identifying and recording personal and professional development needs and planning to meet them.

Self-efficacy: the influence of beliefs on behaviour influenced by verbal encouragement, role modelling and self-modelling.

Transformative learning: the process of changing beliefs, attitudes and values in response to the acquisition of knowledge. Sometimes seen as the main goal of adult learning.

Unconditional positive regard: an unevaluative, warm acceptance and liking of the student as a person

Key terms mostly related to relationship development

Altruism: a benevolent concern for others, selflessness. Whether or not genuine altruism exists has been hotly contested; some argue that ulterior motives of self-interest hide behind altruism.

Boundaries: a border or perimeter of a psychological entity, sometimes crossed without awareness. The phrase 'boundary management' is used by psychoanalysts.

Emotional intelligence: the ability to use emotions for human connection. This is another contested term which frequently includes concepts of self-awareness, an ability to read others' feelings and emotional resilience.

Friend: a person whose company one finds pleasurable, who reinforces self-esteem.

Trust: a confident attitude towards another person which can arise from experience and which can imply knowledge, affection, respect and/or reverence. Personal disclosure can build interpersonal trust.

Chapter 9

How to write like an academic

How do we come to understand what academic writing is?

We all go on a journey when we learn how to write, and this section tries to identify some of the key stages in that journey. In Lee (2018b) I put them in a flow chart to try to get some chronological order, but this is necessarily generic and these issues will not necessarily be experienced by any one researcher or in this order.

Figure 9.1 identifies some key elements in academic writing. These may be altered to suit particular disciplines or genres or even individual student's preferences, but the aim of producing such a flow chart is to give you a toolkit for identifying where you are in understanding what academic writing can mean.

In the same book by Carter and Laurs (2018, pp. 30–39) I explored this in a little more detail.

Words on a page

This refers to an early and naïve conception of academic writing. There is little understanding of plagiarism, rigour or verifiability and anyone's words that are relevant to the topic can be included in roughly any order. There may be an understanding of the need for a beginning, middle and a conclusion, but even that might be a cultural demand that is foreign to some.

Stream of consciousness

here I have borrowed the phrase frequently used to describe the approach to writing of the early twentieth-century author, Virginia Woolf. There is an increased introspection and self-awareness about writing at this stage (as well as a desire to have a comfortable space in which to write, 'a room of one's own'). There is a tendency to be highly self-critical and this can mark a time when students find it difficult to write anything because they feel that everything they do is inadequate. It also marks the beginning of a later stage which is about 'finding your voice'.

Figure 9.1 A chronological approach to elements of academic writing

A structured exercise

There is a growing understanding of the need for structure. It might be to understand the Anglo-American idea of how an essay is expected to be written, or it might be an understanding that another form of skeleton is needed. At this stage a supervisor or advisor might be looking to identify sub-headings, chapter headings or key themes for each paragraph. They will also need to emphasise the importance of keeping a file of references and some form of reference management system.

Writing is reading

There are two main reasons for encouraging reading. First, there is a need for the candidate to master the knowledge base needed to carry out the research, and here conceptualising the literature survey is key. In some countries and in some professional doctorates this first 'mastery of knowledge' phase of the doctorate is examined and assessed before the candidate is allowed to proceed. The second reason for encouraging reading is more of a cultural one – encouraging students to understand how writing is undertaken within a particular discipline (or disciplines – in a multi-disciplinary world) and how writing is undertaken in different countries, particularly the country of the language that the thesis is to be written in.

Style and use of language

Some supervisors struggle with their own writing when it comes to aspects of writing relating to grammar or even the use of words. A heavy reliance on the grammar and spell checkers available within computerised systems does not deal comprehensively with an inadequate or incorrect terminology or use of language. Some text books such as Swales and Feak (2004), Strunk and White (2011) or the classic by Fowler (Burchfield, 1996) can help both advisors and doctoral candidates identify and work on problem areas.

Using feedback

As many have observed, writing is usually a social (as well as a socialised) process. The art of encouraging and using critical feedback is something that all doctoral students need to understand. It is part of the academic endeavour to seek out criticism, preferably before a publisher rejects a piece or an examiner fails it! A dialogue between supervisors and researchers to manage expectations about how much feedback and when it can be expected is important. Equally, opening up researchers' awareness of other sources of feedback is important (for example, can they engage in journal clubs or give and receive feedback from peer groups?).

Writing as perspiration

Closely linked to the idea of getting feedback is the understanding that academic writing is about rewriting, rewriting and rewriting. Sometimes this notion helps overcome the fears associated with writer's block, because the idea that what you first put on the page is never going to be good enough can free people up to start writing something. Rowena Murray (2011) has published many ideas around generative writing and implicit in this approach is a requirement for constant editing.

Identifying your voice

This stage links the formulation of the researcher's identity (possibly their identity as an academic) with an understanding of perspective, the audience and the eventual place of the research. As Kamler and Thomson argue, identity is plural (we have many and evolving identities) and identity is a performance (2006, pp. 16–17). As the writer begins to embrace an ontological perspective, so their voice becomes clearer. The supervisor will be asking 'who are you writing for?', 'what do you want them to believe?' and 'what do you want them to believe about you?'

Writing as research

By now the accumulation of all the above elements is leading to a comprehension of the formulation of original knowledge: whether the author believes original knowledge is an incremental step in our understanding or a major reformulation and reframing of an idea will be becoming apparent. Inherent in the idea of writing as research is the proposition that research is only valuable if it is communicated in some way. There will need to be discussions about intellectual property, patents, copyright and creative commons licencing at this stage.

Formulation of publishable research

At a doctoral level there are many definitions of 'publishable'. The ambition to publish several papers in an international peer-reviewed journal with a high impact factor is more talked about than reality. The threads of writing as a social activity are picked up again here when discussions about co-publishing and co-authorship need to happen. The medical profession has promoted the Vancouver protocol and many others have used it as a lever for negotiation over authorship. It states:

> All persons designated as authors should qualify for authorship. Each author should have participated sufficiently in the work to take public responsibility for the content. Authorship credit should be based only on substantial contributions to
>
> 1)   conception and design, or analysis and interpretation of data; and to
> 2)   drafting the article or revising it critically for important intellectual content; and on
> 3)   final approval of the version to be published.
>
> Conditions 1, 2, and 3 must all be met. Participation solely in the acquisition of funding or the collection of data does not justify authorship. General supervision of the research group is not sufficient for authorship. Any part of an article critical to its main conclusions must be the responsibility of at least one author.
>
> (www.research.mq.edu.au/documents/policies/Vancouver.pdf)

Different disciplines have very different protocols in their publications. In some cases authors are always cited in alphabetical order; in others the first and last named authors are generally recognised as having made the most substantive input; and in other cases it might be the first and second named authors who are most prominent. Understanding these, sometimes implicit, rules is an important part of learning to negotiate (and renegotiate) one's place in the authorial hierarchy. Where it becomes even more complex is when we have interdisciplinary teams publishing together.

Writing as power

Publishing research is in itself an insufficient objective. As many research councils and ethics committees are now demanding, there has to be some awareness of the potential use and impact of the research. Here the opportunity for research to change the world needs to be explored. We assume that the message has been ethically and rigorously arrived at, and how it is conveyed and to whom (finding your voice and adapting it to write for different cultures, disciplines and audiences) becomes the key objective. The written word has the power to outlast any single conference presentation and it creates the opportunity for reflective examination and testing. It can be built upon as part of a life's work.

Combining two frameworks

Table 9.1 describes what researchers and supervisors might be seeking to achieve through their writing up of research and through the doctoral process. They might be seeking any combination of these factors at any time during the process, and that is what makes supervision and advising such an interesting and challenging process.

A researcher operating from a *functional* position will be focusing on the number of words required, formatting, how documents should be presented and whether or not deadlines are being met (including whether or not they receive feedback from their supervisor within an agreed time).

A student focusing more on *enculturation* will be looking to be part of the research or academic community. They will want to be invited to research seminars, journal clubs and conferences. They will be keen to steep themselves in the literature that is relevant to their topic and important in the department. Feedback on their writing from peers and colleagues will be eagerly sought.

This is different to the candidate who is operating from the *critical thinking* approach, for whom enquiry becomes almost an obsession. They will be constantly asking themselves the question closely associated with the philosopher, Karl Popper, 'in how many ways could I be wrong?' They will be looking for fallacious assertions hidden in the written word; they will want to identify inconsistencies, questionable assumptions and will seek to see a strong thread uniting a coherent argument in any piece of work.

As we have seen before, enculturation contrasts particularly strongly with *emancipation*, and this is still true when looking at how the writing up of research is supervised. The student who is seeking an emancipated approach from their supervisor may react strongly against the imposition of what they may see as artificial deadlines, rigid disciplinary conventions and forced submission to 'esteemed' journals. Cotterall (2011) and Hirvela and Yi (2008) observe how a student's identity changes when they learn to write at this level, and recognising this is often an important element of the emancipatory approach, as is exploring the student's motivation to write (Murray, 2011). In this approach the student needs time to experiment (and this can be frustrating for your supervisor). The difficulty here is an article of faith: is your wide-ranging reading helping to formulate an innovative project with new ways of expressing themselves, or is it just timewasting and filibustering? Writing up as you go will give you some evidence to make an assessment here.

In the *relationship development* approach the student wants to feel that their writing is personally valued and to exchange ideas about how to cope with writing challenges. Some of the questions raised by students and their advisors under each approach are summarised in Table 9.1.

We can extend and test this framework against the chronological elements of the researcher's understanding of the academic writing process as described in Figure 9.1 (above). So if you are at stage 1 (believing that writing is just about getting the words down on the page), you might use any of the five approaches (functional, enculturation, critical thinking, emancipation, relationship development), or any combination of the approaches, to move yourself on to the next stage. For example you bring a popular magazine article on the topic and contrast it with an academic journal's article (enculturation).

Table 9.2 is intended to show how the framework of five approaches can create new ways of looking at supervising writing. If you can identify the stage that you are at, then you can read across the table to get a range of suggestions for helping you to move on to the next stage.

Enabling writing at this most advanced level is an essential part of becoming a successful doctoral writer. For many academics, words are the central tool of their trade, and focusing on how to craft them and what they mean both epistemologically and ontologically is both an exciting and central part of creating an original research project.

Each of these tasks can be further defined, varied, combined and extended. All of these examples and those in Tables 9.3 and 9.4 below can contribute to the production of a thesis and enable student learning through writing.

> This array of tasks shows the range of writing activities that is possible and, implicitly, explains the many different purposes of 'writing' whilst doing research: writing to develop ideas, writing to find focus, writing to explain focus, writing to explain the research, writing to make the case for the research, writing to document ideas and writing (that is much-revised) ready to submit for assessment or peer review. These different purposes call for different writing activities. Writing retreats (a period of dedicated time when writers work in the same place, separate from other research tasks) are considered as a separate part of the table because the fact that aspects of such retreats can be allocated to each approach explains why they can create such a powerful experience (Murray and Cunningham

Table 9.1 The questions raised by different approaches to supervising academic writing

Functional	Enculturation	Critical thinking	Emancipation	Relationship development
Are there sufficient words or number of pages completed?	What does the peer feedback say?	Does the argument have a logical thread?	Why is this piece of work important to you? What personal values are exposed by this work?	Will the supervisor/student approve of and like what has been written?
What is the correct formatting and presentation?	Publishing in journals esteemed by colleagues	Is the argument convincing?	How can the underlying message be made powerful?	Can I trust my co-author to be ethical in their research?
Are deadlines going to be met?	Referencing key authors in the discipline	In how many ways can the argument be disproved/criticised? Have contradictory views been acknowledged?	How is this piece of writing changing or challenging the author?	What experiences can we share that will help the student overcome challenges?

Table 9.2 A chronological approach to elements of academic writing extended by analysis through the framework of five approaches to research supervision

	Functional	Enculturation	Critical thinking	Emancipation	Relationship development
Words on the page	Do a short writing task to prompts set by the supervisor	Explore the difference between popular and academic articles	Discuss as much of the 'chronological elements' as you think appropriate	Use a prompt to write generatively on the topic	Share your passion for the topic or research methods
Stream of consciousness	Write anything on the topic for five minutes	Look at popular writers on the topic	Encourage reflective writing (theorising from experience)	Freewriting (see Murray, 2011)	Discuss own understanding of academic reflection
A structured exercise	Get a series of headings to write to	Look at headings in other's theses and journal articles. Share referees' reports	Analyse the purpose and place of structure. Encourage precision	Compare writing with and without structure	Take a piece of your own writing and reveal its inner structure
Writing is reading	Read journal articles	Look at good examples of literature reviews to read	Look at how literature reviews are structured	Read about students' doctoral journeys	Share your reading and note-taking strategies

(Continued)

Table 9.2 (Cont.)

	Functional	Enculturation	Critical thinking	Emancipation	Relationship development
Style and use of language	Attend generic writing courses	Get peers to review your writing style and offer to review theirs	Analyse the style of great writers, e.g. Bertrand Russell	Read widely	Share reading work out loud so that you can stop and discuss key points
Using feedback	Establish an agreement with your supervisor about getting timely feedback before you submit anything. Keep records of feedback given	Attend journal clubs, present work at seminars and conferences etc.	Explore the role of feedback in developing critical thinking	Discuss what you find most helpful from feedback. Look at whether you are really using the feedback you are given	Share how you have dealt with receiving difficult feedback in the past. Get feedback verbally (face to face) and in writing
Writing as perspiration	Look at time management to ensure time is available for rewriting	Look at the careers of successful academics in your field	Analyse the processes involved in getting to a completed piece of work	Discuss how to cope with tiredness, boredom and failure	Share your own writing and rewriting experiences
Identifying your voice	Are there any important academic conventions,	Identify who the critical readers are for this research and	Discuss how we can identify who the audience is likely to	Identify when you are 'in flow' writing	Describe how your own inner voice works when you are writing

	e.g. using first or third person	what is most likely to influence them	be for any given piece of work		
Writing as research	Set a project plan and timetable	Chart the evolution of thought through key articles in your subject	Look at what can be considered to be original knowledge	Explore how you formulate your ideas	Share first and final drafts of articles you have written
Fomulation of publishable research	Set or negotiate a publications plan	Discuss authorship policies in your department/discipline. Look at key journals to seek publication in	Formulate a strategy for publishing work	Discuss whether or not publication is important to you	Reveal the impact that publishing your work has had
Writing as power	Discuss what you mean by power. Set objectives and create a plan to realise them	Look at the careers that successful researchers in your field have subsequently undertaken	Probe the values that are important to the researcher	Look at the role of autonomy in research	Share any ethical concerns that you have

2011). Whilst all of the activities included in the tables in this chapter are well established in the field of academic writing, they are likely to be less generally familiar.

(Lee & Murray, 2015, p. 564)

Writing in English as an additional language

Research, especially at the doctoral level, is increasingly an international and an interdisciplinary exercise. The use of any language other than one's mother tongue(s) requires a deep cultural understanding as well as a good memory and significant effort. To write in English, at the highest academic level that we know of, is not a task for the faint-hearted, whatever the author's first language. However, the cultural capital that is acquired by being able to write in a second or subsequent language conveys a significant advantage.

EAL researchers will become more valuable citizens and possibly more valuable employees because of their mastery of different languages and cultures. However, there are some aspects of writing that we particularly need to be sure are explicit. These include:

- ways of articulating arguments
- views about the construction of knowledge and validity
- institutional practices and support about plagiarism, literacy and proofreading
- ways of presenting the thesis.

Lu, Li and Ottowell (2016) and Ottowell (2018) argue that the most difficult barrier that international postgraduate students face is 'contrastic or intercultural rhetoric'. By this they mean different cultural understandings about what makes a powerful argument. They define rhetoric as being concerned with 'factors of analysis, data gathering, interpretation and synthesis' (Ottowell, 2018, p. 23). In a study of first-language Mandarin speakers they identified that native speakers use many more linking words and phrases (such as 'however', 'in spite of', 'as a result of'). They argue that these linking words and phrases are important in creating a persuasive argument in Western culture. There are other linking words or phrases that Chinese-speaking students are more likely to use and some phrases that are frequently confused.

This is an important piece of research to be aware of. If this is a need then there are various ways of dealing with it. There are three examples of solutions that could be considered here:

- referral to learning advisors
- taking individual tuition from the supervisor
- using handouts or resources (such as the Manchester Academic Phrasebank: www.phrasebank.manchester.ac.uk/).

Table 9.3 An initial range of issues for EAL students to consider

Functional	Enculturation	Critical thinking	Emancipation	Relationship development
Go to astudent advisor specialising in supporting academic writing for international students (sometimes found in the library) Use resources such as the Manchester University Academic Phrasebank	Can you describe your argument as you would do it in your first language and as you would make it in English? What are the differences?	Compare the structure of an introduction with typical academic moves, for example: 1 Demonstrating why the current research is important 2 Indicating a gap or need 3 Indicating the main findings	Self-assess your work. Read it out loud in English and then describe the support that you would find most helpful Use Table 9.4 to assess what would be most helpful to you	Seek individual one-to-one tuition Be alert to any additional stress you might be under while mastering this skill and seek support if necessary

Specific examples will help all students, and are often particularly sought after by those working in an additional language. Paltridge and Starfield (2007) offer a good range of them organised in a chronological sequence from the introduction to the conclusion.

Good practice in feedback on research writing

In Table 9.4 I explore in more detail different types of feedback that you might seek. It is particularly important to establish an understanding about the relative importance of each of these issues so that you can find the best source of such advice. Some of the options are more easily discussed individually and many of them can usefully be discussed with small groups of students.

Other common problems that students face when writing up their research include: writing in a circumlocutory manner; poor grammar and sentence structure; writer's block; revising work as their advisor requests but not showing any further initiative; summarising but not conceptualising the literature; asking for excessive help with rewriting; and not submitting work to an agreed deadline. Any of these problems can arise for both an international and a local candidate, and all of them can be managed by utilising a combination of approaches to doing research.

Choosing publications to submit to

Countries, universities, disciplines, departments and supervisors all have differing views about the virtue of writing for publication during a research project. In general, if you are realistically seeking an academic career then having some publications on your CV will help, but some supervisors have good reasons for preferring that their student concentrates on the actual research and completing the project before aiming for publication. In some groups so many people are involved in a research project that publication is as much a matter of negotiating authorial order as it is contributing written material.

Whether or not you chooses to publish, and where and when this might happen, requires careful thought. It can be enormously motivating to see your work in print, but there are many options to consider and it is important to consider timing and any intellectual property considerations first. Table 9.5 lists a wide range of publishing options for consideration. Not every piece of research needs to be submitted to a prestigious journal such as *Nature* and the creative supervisor will consider a wide range of options for students doing research at all stages of the curriculum. Table 9.5 is not in order of importance, but some are obviously more suitable for undergraduate research than others. It shows what a wide range of options there can be and all have very different types of readers in mind. Each option has an impact on employability (for good or for bad), so needs to be considered from this point of view as well. The student who chooses video or sound media will appeal strongly to some

Table 9.4 What students might be seeking from feedback on academic writing

Functional	Enculturation	Critical thinking	Emancipation	Relationship development
1 Timely and clear feedback	1 Consistent feedback offered	1 A balance of critique and constructive comments	1 Recognition that the work is the student's responsibility	1 A partnership of equals, not a manager–employee relationship
2 Help with structure and organisation	2 Help with finding literature	2 Help with identifying irrelevances or condensing material	2 Suggestions, but not too directive	2 Written feedback first, then a meeting to discuss it face to face
3 Help with grammar, spelling and punctuation	3 Help with appropriate language, e.g. 'this language is too informal'	3 Ability to critique own work		3 Supervisor to demonstrate genuine interest in student's work and well-being
4 Structure in receiving feedback, e.g. supervisor always provides an overview and then more detailed comments on the script	4 Help with appropriate methodology			

Table 9.5 A range of publishing options

Type of publication	Key issues
University newspaper/blog	Easier to contact editors Easier to identify readers' interest
Own blog/vlog	Popular, easy to set up, time-consuming to maintain, not always frequently accessed by readers so marketing it becomes an issue Difficult to eradicate if student changes their mind
Supervisor-curated collection	Supervisor needs to manage circulation Supervisor needs to manage editing
Local newspaper/ blog/vlog	Contemporary, relevant, may have local impact but be limited in terms of longevity
National newspaper/ blog/vlog	Contemporary, relevant, may have national impact but be limited in terms of longevity
Professional journals	Can have considerable impact in different employment contexts
Reports	Commissioned reports for professional bodies, lobbyists, management groups, governments or policy developers can be an important way of getting research results into the legislative mainstream
Conference proceedings	Useful after a conference presentation; need to calibrate publication according to strength of material
Academic journals	Can take a long time to achieve publication, peer review can enhance quality, some seminal articles have a long life Co-authorship issues need careful consideration Impact on academic profession can be high
Book chapters	Edited chapters can provide essential sourcebooks for many readers
Book/monograph	Longer life than many other publications, room to expand a thesis and develop a train of thought, but takes a great deal of time to write Self-publishing and crowd-funding options are increasing and will have differing types of impact

employers, while the candidate who successfully pursues the academic journal will be enhancing their appeal to universities or research institutes. In many cases co-authorship is possible, and it is worth negotiating who is going to contribute what and the order in which authors will be credited from the beginning (bearing in mind the disciplinary conventions and/or the Vancouver protocol).

Whenever a student doing research is considering publishing their work there are some very fundamental questions that you need to ensure have been addressed (Becker & Denicolo, 2012). It could take at least one supervision session to work through them all, and any of your co-supervisors involved in the project should probably be included in this discussion as well. A summary of the questions for discussion are listed in Box 9.1. Question 7 can be particularly complex because a publication plan (where publication in several journals or places is part of a longer-term ambition) needs to avoid accusations of 'salami slicing' (where the actual information presented has only a minor difference between one journal and the next) and 'self-plagiarising' where the author unnecessarily repeats themselves through referencing and quoting previous work.

Box 9.1 Questions to address if publication is sought

1 Who is my reader? Why will they care about my research?
2 What is my key message?
3 How many different journals/types of publication might I consider? What are the advantages and disadvantages of each?
4 Who are the gatekeepers to this form of publication (e.g. editors) and can I get any more information from them about structure, formatting, timetables and what they would consider acceptable?
5 What sort of articles have been published in this journal/medium before? Does this affect how I portray my message or does it affect the message itself?
6 Are there any special editions or key events coming up that are going to make my research particularly timely?
7 Will publishing in my chosen forum preclude publishing elsewhere, or does it build a platform for further publications?
8 What style does this journal/medium tend to prefer?
9 How many words/minutes am I aiming for?
10 How long will it take me to write this? How will it affect the progress of my research?
11 How might publication affect my CV or future career opportunities?

Rejection emails are a part of life for academics. Depending on the content in the rejection, we can either use it (or some of it) as a guideline for rewriting, or we can reconsider who our audience should be for this type of work. Contradictory feedback is not unusual, and if you are making an argument for resubmission, pointing out the contradictions to the editor (in a fair and balanced manner) as part of your resubmission can be helpful.

In this chapter I have explored the stages that a researcher might move through in developing their understanding of academic writing, then related these stages to the five approaches so that you can identify which stage you might be at and then choose an appropriate approach for moving on. There is a growing body of advice for supervisors of students who are writing in an additional language, and key parts of that advice are summarised here. We also look at different approaches to publishing during or after a research project. In the next chapter we look at dilemmas and some of the issues raised when working with co-supervisors or a supervisory team.

Further reading

Sword, H. (2012) *Stylish academic writing.* Boston, MA: Harvard University Press.

Chapter 10

Dilemmas

When you disagree with your supervisor(s)

It has become the norm for a student doing doctoral-level research to have at least two supervisors. The configuration varies: your co-supervisor can be an academic point of contact for emergencies only, or an important part of the team. The co-supervisor might even be your main supervisor in all but name. There can be co-supervisors working on different campuses, even in different countries, and for some professional doctorates a co-supervisor can be an external advisor, not an academic but a gatekeeper to data or financial resources who is resident in a different workplace. All of these configurations offer opportunities for power play (Manathunga, 2012) and point to the need for a neutral language and tools that you can all use to explore how to use your strengths to become successful.

One of the most distressing experiences for students doing research is to find that their supervisors strongly disagree over a key point. Of course, this creates a learning opportunity, but it is better if it is used as such rather than a battleground between supervisors.

The importance of 'negotiating roles, expectations, timelines and communication protocols' is made clear in establishing a relationship of trust (Manathunga, 2017, p. 4). Without such negotiation there is a risk of innocent but slightly thoughtless actions (such as engaging in writing for publication without the knowledge of others in the team) escalating into a loss of trust across the team. Where professional trust is established there are resilient teams who empower students. In the next section we explore different ways of establishing trust in supervisory teams: negotiating responsibilities, empowering students, making the most of differing approaches, sample case studies for departmental discussion and using the five approaches to summarise different ways of establishing and recognising trust.

Enabling understanding across research teams: making the best of differing approaches

As I have said before, the most useful table in this book for establishing trust is Table 7.5: Establishing a good relationship from the beginning.

In some supervisory teams the language of the five approaches that runs through this book is well established. In that case it can be used to chart the supervisory team as a whole and to look at where the strengths and weaknesses might be. Either from using the self-assessment questionnaire in Chapter 2 (Table 2.2) or just through discussion, spider diagrams can be created which visually demonstrate where there might be gaps.

In Figure 10.1 we possibly have a nearly perfect team with two supervisors, a graduate school director, a postgraduate administrator and a researcher. All

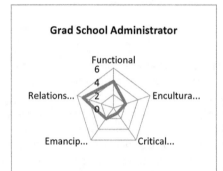

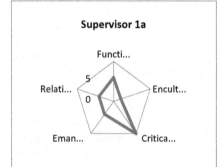
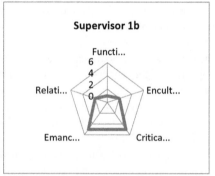
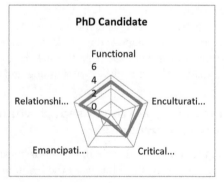

Figure 10.1 Charting a supervisory team

aspects of supervision are covered, but supervisor 1B needs to be aware that they have the greatest interest in supporting the student over compiling the literature review, discipline skill building and any publications to be considered (not a role normally undertaken by the graduate school director – who is strong in enculturation but who will probably be more focused on organising group events). The whole team needs to recognise that the student may need support in meta reflection, reframing and careers decisions (emancipation).

Developing and extending your research team

In Chapter 6 we saw in Table 6.1 a range of people who might be available to support the student doing research. It is important for you to understand the role of the postgraduate administrator in your university – they can be an enormous support for you and may well have seen more students doing research through their projects than any other member of staff. Lab assistants or technicians and subject librarians can also be vital aids to success. Making good relationships with key people from those in the list below might save you considerable time.

Who can be included in your academic support network?

1 Principle supervisor
2 Secondary or co-supervisor
3 Work-based or industrial supervisor
4 Specialist advisors (including post-doctoral researchers)
5 Postgraduate administrator
6 Doctoral candidates/PGRs
7 Postgraduate teaching assistant co-ordinator
8 Lab assistants/technicians
9 Specialist librarians
10 Postgraduate careers advisors
11 Director of postgraduate research/director of postgraduate school
12 Others?

Establishing trust: case studies

An institution and a department has a collective responsibility that goes beyond individual supervisors (McAlpine, 2013), so while this chapter focuses on the relationship between two or more co-supervisors, that should also be seen in a wider context. The culture of the department, school and faculty will also have an impact and a culture where some difficult issues can be aired and problems shared will be a healthier one. One way of enabling non-confrontational dialogue is to have group meetings of supervisors where case studies such as the following are discussed.

Case study 1a: conflicts at a distance

Your co-supervisor is at another university many miles away and rarely can all three of you meet together. At the last meeting one supervisor told you that they thought your analysis so far was too superficial. You said that you had met with the other supervisor only a couple of weeks earlier, and was told then that everything was fine. What can you do now, and how can you stop this happening again?

Case study 1b: conflicts over theory

Your supervisors have significant differences over the theoretical approach that you should take in your research. One believes that the way forward is to use narrative enquiry – as an interview/discussion tool it will enable you to uncover rich material for analysis. Your co-supervisor is very experienced in action research and wants you to set up an action research project. He says that this will enable you to publish work with a demonstrable impact. You sense an impasse and ask both supervisors to agree a route forward so that you know what to do next.

Response

These are common situations and both provide a learning opportunity. Distance can make things more difficult and requires some longer-term planning. In case study 1a is there an opportunity for you to travel to the other supervisor and learning anything there? Below are some ways that the different approaches might help you find an answer.

Case study 2: conflict over co-authorship

You plan to write most of a journal article based on your research. One supervisor has contributed a key idea and the other one has offered to edit it for grammar and use of language. Now you find that both supervisors expect to be named as co-authors. You do not want to upset them, but you are not sure that this is appropriate.

Response

This is one of the most difficult situations of all, but an important one to learn how to manage. Different disciplines and different journals will have conventions that you will have to become familiar with. Some journals now ask each contributor to state clearly what they have done. As we saw in Chapter 9, the Vancouver protocol can be helpful if it applies to your type of work (www .research.mq.edu.au/documents/policies/Vancouver.pdf).

Table 10.1 Some approaches to managing contradictory advice

Functional	Enculturation	Critical thinking	Emancipation	Relationship development
Plan ahead for a joint meeting – Skype or face to face. Consult both on the agenda in advance Are there specialists available in the type of analysis/research that you are doing who can help you further?	Can you review some successful research projects? Can any be recommended where this type of analysis/theory has been used?	Do the supervisors come from different traditions? Might this explain the difference? (See also Chapter 5.) What position will your assessor come from?	Interview both supervisors (perhaps separately) and write up a position paper summarising your recommendations	Request a joint meeting. Quietly but clearly say to both supervisors together that you find it confusing when they espouse contradictory views and ask for their help

Table 10.2 The invisible supervisor – working it through

Functional	Enculturation	Critical thinking	Emancipation	Relationship development
Check with the postgraduate administrator that you are fulfilling all your obligations. Review your Gantt chart with the active supervisor – is everything on track?	Discuss the roles of different supervisors with the active supervisor. Has there been an agreement that Pat will just oversee the formal procedures? Request a mock assessment or second opinion to check that your work is up to standard	Are you getting enough advice and support? If you need more, what are your options? Who can you go to raise this question?	Is everything else proceeding well? Is there a problem? What is the problem? What should happen if the active supervisor is no longer available? Is Pat intended to be just an emergency academic point of contact?	Work through the active supervisor if possible. Request a meeting with your main supervisor or with both supervisors together as appropriate. Send material that you want feedback on well in advance

Table 10.3 Five approaches to building and assessing trust

Functional	Enculturation	Critical thinking	Emancipation	Relationship development
Transactional trust: doing what is agreed on time	Meeting together and sharing work plans Discussing hypothetical case studies together	Trust in academic integrity and rigour Being explicit about who will undertake different responsibilities	Trusting that while the other members of the team are elsewhere they are supporting not undermining your work	Spending time together over coffee or the occasional meal Demonstrating interest in the well-being of the other team members

Part of the art of managing this situation is working out how to prevent it becoming an issue before you go any further. Suggesting you have a meeting with both supervisors where you outline exactly what each is going to contribute and discuss any disciplinary or departmental conventions is the best way forward. Agreeing authorship and co-authorship in advance (while always being open to renegotiation if things change) is better than discussing it later. Remember, there is also a role for acknowledgements in every journal article. If this situation has already arisen, you may need to take advice from someone responsible for ethical research in your institution.

Case study 3: the invisible supervisor

Pat is (on paper) your main supervisor. You have met Pat once in the last 18 months. Pat agreed with all your recommendations and signed the annual review. In passing Pat said to you that you are doing an excellent job, but didn't pause long enough to have a proper discussion. Should you do anything about this, and if so what?

Response

This could be a serious problem or no problem at all. While good practice normally suggests there should be two active supervisors, it is not universal. The way that co-supervisors divide the work up between them varies enormously. The main supervisor may know more than you realise, or might be negligent.

Building and assessing trust in supervisory teams

Academic teams of supervisors and researchers are not going to be perfect. Some of the suggestions for building and assessing trust in Table 10.3 are easier to achieve than others. Each of these approaches to establishing and maintaining trust will reinforce the whole process. Where trust has broken down it might be possible to use this table to identify priorities for development so that it can be re-established.

In this chapter we have looked at a range of tools to help academic teams of researchers and supervisors to work together. There is a great deal of work involved in using these tools, so the wise supervisory team will select the ones that are most useful for their situation. In the next chapter we turn to look at some of the ethical dilemmas that might confront supervisors.

Chapter 11

Preparing for your work to be examined

Within any examined system we are all strategic learners to some extent: we work towards the criteria by which our work is going to be assessed (Biggs & Tang, 2007). So being clear about how work is going to be examined and assessed is an important part of the research project. There are some matters that are still a matter of academic judgement, such as whether a piece of work contains a sufficient contribution to original knowledge (see Chapter 1 for examples of qualification frameworks and below for examples of definitions of a contribution to original knowledge), and there are some procedures that you will need to find out about because they vary in different institutions and countries.

Even though this is almost the last chapter in the book, it still contains data that is probably available in the student handbooks that you were given at the beginning of your programme. Referring to the guidelines in them many months before you have to submit is wise.

Managing the last few minutes before the submission deadline

Most written work is now submitted digitally. Submitting via plagiarism software and proofreading is required, so you will need to make sure you have left plenty of time for this. Most universities are rigorous about expecting work to be submitted on time, often closing a submission window on the appointed hour, so always allow time for computer problems and internet failings. It is always safer to avoid being in a position where you are submitting at the last minute.

Creating rubrics for assessment at different curriculum levels

Most programme teams will have agreed assessment criteria for marking projects at undergraduate and master's levels. Rubrics are a way of enabling (more) common marking standards and equity. In this section we will look at examples of such rubrics for assessing written work and see if one can usefully be created for assessing doctoral-level theses. It is not only what is in the rubric, but also how it is used that is important.

One such rubric was created and explored by academics teaching on a Dutch BA Educational Science programme. It had four levels and levels 2–4 were passes. In Table 11.1 we look at excerpts from a rubric that was used after the first revision (Prins, de Kleijn & van Tartwijk, 2017).

Prins's team suggested that rubrics can be used as a teacher assessment tool, for increasing student awareness of criteria and for supporting peer feedback or self-assessment. You can certainly use a rubric to assess your own work, but they did warn that it is only appropriate for peer assessment in some situations and if it is used in that way there needs to be careful management of the situation.

At master's level similar (but obviously more sophisticated) tools can be used. In Table 11.2 is a rubric that was used for assessing work submitted for a 'Teaching in Higher Education' qualification. The table has been adapted from a document by Price and Rust, which was originally published by the Higher Education Academy but no longer available. It needs to be amended further by readers to reflect more of the research carried out in different disciplinary contexts.

Table 11.1 Excerpts from a rubric for BA Educational Science

	Level 2 – must have	Level 3 – good	Level 4 – points of excellence
Introduction methods	Explains why this problem is important, relevant literature introduced, variables operationally defined	Makes clear this is an important contribution to the field Information provided enables replication	Original approach Analyses outside the curriculum
Results discussion	Results used to address the research question	Limitations of results taken into account	New literature, outstanding practical relevance
Organisation of manuscript	Organised, coherent structure, APA referencing style, language clear and precise	Continuity in words, concepts and thematic development Tables and figures clear	Written in English (this paper came from the Netherlands)
Process	Meets commitments, deadlines and is polite Responds to and processes supervisor's feedback	Asks for help, support and instruction and provides relevant and concrete questions	Self-proposed solutions Outstanding willingness to learn

Table 11.2 Sample marking criteria for written submissions for a master's programme

	Criterion	A	B+	B	C	Refer/fail
1	Presentation of assignment. Conforming with instructions (e.g. word length). Clear expression, accurate spelling and grammar	Shows a polished and imaginative approach to the topic. Work submitted in time and within prescribed parameters. Fluent writing, accurate spelling and grammar	Carefully and logically organised. Work submitted in time and within prescribed parameters. Accurate spelling and grammar	Shows organisation and coherence. Work submitted in time and within prescribed parameters. Mainly accurate spelling and grammar	Shows some attempt to organise in a logical manner. Deviates slightly from the required parameters. Meaning apparent but some grammar and spelling errors	Disorganised/incoherent. Work submitted late with no allowable reason and deviates from required parameters. Meaning unclear. Frequent errors
2	Attention to purpose	Has addressed the purpose of the assignment comprehensively and imaginatively	Has addressed the purpose of the assignment coherently and with some attempt to demonstrate imagination	Has addressed the main purpose of the assignment	Some of the work is focused on the aims and themes of the assignment	Fails to address the task set
3	Content, range and knowledge of theory	Comprehensive/detailed knowledge of topic with areas of specialisation in depth and awareness of provisional nature of knowledge. Innovative use of theory	Reasonable knowledge of topic and an awareness of a variety of ideas/contexts/frameworks. Insightful and appropriate selection of theory in key areas	Has given a factual and/or conceptual knowledge base and appropriate terminology. Most key theories are included appropriately	Evidence of limited knowledge of topic and some use of appropriate terminology. Some appropriate theory selected, not always correctly used	Lacks evidence of knowledge relevant to the topic and/or significantly misuses terminology. Inaccurate or inappropriate theory
4	Use of literature/evidence of reading	Has developed and justified using own ideas based on a wide range of sources which have been thoroughly	Able to critically appraise the literature and theory gained from variety of sources,	Clear evidence and application of readings relevant to the subject; uses	Literature is presented uncritically, in a purely descriptive way and	Either no evidence of literature being consulted or

(Continued)

Table 11.2 (Cont).

	Criterion	A	B+	B	C	Refer/fail
		analysed, applied and discussed	developing own ideas in the process	indicative texts identified	indicates limitations of understanding	irrelevant to the assignment set
5	Disciplinarity and context in which subject is used	Takes account of disciplinarity, complex contexts and selects appropriate technique	Takes some account of discipline, contexts and selects some appropriate techniques	Recognises discipline boundaries, defines context and uses standard techniques for that discipline	Context acknowledged but not really taken into account	Context not recognised as relevant
6	Conclusions	Analytical and clear conclusions well-grounded in theory and literature showing development of new concepts	Good development shown in summary of arguments based in theory/literature	Evidence of findings and conclusions grounded in theory/literature	Limited evidence of findings and conclusions supported by theory/literature	Unsubstantiated/invalid conclusions based on anecdote and generalisation only, or no conclusions at all
7	Reflection/evaluation	Metacognition evident. Is confident in application of own criteria of judgement and in challenge of received opinion. Can critically review evidence supporting conclusions/recommendations, including its validity	Is able to evaluate own strengths and weaknesses; can challenge received opinion and begins to develop own criteria and judgement. Can use a variety of sources for reflection and evaluation and can evaluate the relevance and significance of data collected	Is largely dependent on criteria set by others but begins to recognise own strengths and weaknesses. Can stand back from the event and evaluate the reliability of data using defined techniques and/or tutor guidance	Dependent on criteria set by others. Begins to recognise own strengths and weakness. Limited and only partially accurate reflection and evaluation of data using defined techniques and/or tutor guidance	Fails to meaningfully undertake the process of self-criticism. Fails to evaluate or use techniques of evaluation, or evaluations are totally invalid

The final part of this section includes a rubric or marking criteria that may be helpful for assessing a research thesis. It is adapted from a longer document (Lovitts, 2007) and needs critical engagement because it is so generic. Some academics would argue that only the 'outstanding' column is acceptable at doctoral level, but even then the examiners need to discuss this before embarking upon the assessment process.

How can we recognise 'an original contribution to knowledge'?

There are three key aspects to ensuring that a contribution can be defined as original. Not all of the second point needs to be demonstrated at once. Indeed, we would normally expect only one aspect to be used to defend a doctoral thesis. From work by Wellington (2013), Clarke and Lunt (2014) and Trafford and Leshem (2008), the following may help to clarify a definition of an original contribution to knowledge at doctoral level.

1 **Publishable:** meaning worthy of peer-reviewed publication and takes account of previously published work on the subject.
2 **Significant novel contribution:** meaning it presents a significant contribution to learning, for example through the discovery of new knowledge, the connection of previously unrelated facts, the development of new theory or the revision of older views. It may build new knowledge by extending previous work or 'putting a new brick in the wall'; it may use original processes, create a new synthesis, explore new implications for practitioners, policy makers or theorists; it might revise a recurrent issue or debate by offering new evidence, thinking or theory and it might replicate or reproduce earlier work but applied to a different place or time with a different sample. Finally, it needs to be authentic – the student's own work.
3 **Systematic:** meaning it forms a coherent body of work.

Summary of different definitions of an original contribution to knowledge.

In different disciplines you could argue that any of the following characteristics would constitute an original contribution to knowledge. It is unlikely that a doctoral thesis is going to be 'ground-breaking' or 'change how a field is viewed', but this is a very useful list to refer to when you are asked to defend or describe what is original about your work.

1 New methods on old data/context or old methods on new data/context
2 Incremental development or change
3 Recognises significant research problems and states gap in knowledge

Table 11.3 What makes a good, bad or outstanding thesis? Some suggestions

Dimensions of the task	Outstanding	Very good	Acceptable	Unacceptable
Introduction	Presents a compelling problem/ research question and indicates why it is significant and important	Poses a good question	Orientates reader to a problem	Does not state the problem, or trivialises it
Literature review	Justifies criteria for inclusion and exclusion	Some discussion of criteria for inclusion or exclusion		Partial coverage Does not discuss criteria for inclusion or exclusion
	Distinguishes what has been done in the field from what needs to be done	Some critical examination of the state of the field, some understanding of the history of literature in the field		Accepts literature at face value History of the field not discussed
	Identifies ambiguities Synthesises and offers a new perspective on the field	Reviews relationships among key variables Some conceptualisation		Description, little synthesis
Methodology and methods	Identifies main methodologies and research methods that have been used in the field. Demonstrates understanding of philosophical perspective. Embraces an ontological perspective	Critiques research methods. Discusses practical and scholarly significance of methods used. Demonstrates epistemic understanding		Research methods and philosophical perspective not discussed

	Uses state-of-the-art tools, techniques or approaches. Uses multiple methods	Uses existing methods correctly and creatively. Discusses why method was chosen	Appropriate for the problem. Provides sufficient documentation	Uses wrong or inappropriate methods. Methods do not relate to the question or theory. Method is fatally flawed
Results/analysis	Original, powerful, sophisticated, robust. Provides plausible interpretations, discusses limitations	Produces rich, high-quality data. Substantiates results	Analysis is objective, aligns with question and theory, but based on a small amount of data/ interpretation too simplistic	Analysis is wrong, inappropriate or incompetent. Cannot discern what is important or explain results. Makes improper inferences
Discussion and conclusion	Short, clear, concise. Refers back to introduction. Identifies significance and contribution. Places work in wider context	Provides a good summary. Ties everything together. Discusses limitations. Identifies some future directions	Summarises what has been accomplished, does not address the significance of the research or place it in context. Identifies a few non-specific next steps	Inadequate or misleading. Repeats the introduction. Does not understand the results of what has been done

4   Recognised by peers (published and peer reviewed)
5   Slightly different twist on a topic
6   Generates new insights
7   Changing how the field is viewed
8   Ground-breaking.

Clarke and Lunt (2014) interviewed, surveyed and observed examiners and candidates and argue that 'originality' and 'a contribution to knowledge' need to be disentangled. They may also mean different things in different disciplines. They introduce two additional issues for assessment: the concept of integrity as a researcher and the ability to communicate and defend results.

Assessment of research takes many forms, even at the doctoral level. In Scandinavia the public defence can be more of a ritual because peer-reviewed publication is often essential before a thesis can go forward for examination and a university committee will decide whether or not the thesis can go forward for defence. In Australia the external examiners will compile detailed written reports because travelling across time zones is problematic. In the UK a *viva* will be conducted face to face with two or three examiners interviewing the student sometimes over several hours. At master's and undergraduate level there still may be an additional oral assessment of a written dissertation and it is important at all levels that students are prepared for the types of assessment criteria that will be applied. The UK system allows for formative feedback because, if the work is basically good enough, corrections can be made after the *viva* and before the award is made. Other systems do not allow for this process although there are calls for it to happen (Kumar & Stracke, 2018).

The importance of mock examinations

Whether or not formative feedback is built into the system, rehearsal for the final assessment is an important part of the supervision process. A practice presentation, mock *viva* or a mock defence can be used to bolster self-confidence. It can also be helpful to have highlighted any areas that need more work before the thesis is submitted. There is a video of one type of *viva* made at the University of Cardiff available for viewing at http://vimeo.com/29731605

Box 11.1 Some questions for the defence/*viva*

CHOICE OF TOPIC/MOTIVATION

1   Why did you choose this topic for your doctorate?
2   How did you get into this area?
3   What are you most proud of?

UNDERSTANDING THE FIELD

4   How would you compare your work to that done by X?
5   How would you characterise your approach to research?
6   How would you justify your choice of methodology?
7   How did you arrive at your conceptual framework?

RESEARCH METHODS

8   How did you design your research?
9   How do you compare your chosen methods with others available?
10 Why did you decide to use XYZ as your main instrument(s)?
11 How did you select your respondents/material/area?
12 How did you arrive at your conceptual conclusions?

IMPLICATIONS

13 How generalisable are your findings and why?
14 Public perception, impact: what use can this work be put to?
15 How will you take your findings back to your sample?
16 What is your main contribution to knowledge?
17 We would like you to critique your thesis for us.

FUTURE PLANS

18 What are you going to do after you gain your doctorate?

FEEDBACK FOR THE UNIVERSITY

19 When supervisor is not present, or has withdrawn: this is your
    chance to comment on the supervision you received. Your com-
    ments will be fed back to the university.

FINALLY

20 Is there anything else you could tell us about your thesis which you
    have not had the opportunity to tell us during the *viva*?

Table 11.4 Preparing for assessment

Functional	Enculturation	Critical thinking	Emancipation	Relationship development
Ensure that you understand as much as possible about the assessment criteria	Try to get other students or an academic who has not been closely involved in your work to review it	Explore the implications of the assessment criteria early on	Pre-assess your own work and identify how secure you feel about your judgement	Organise friends and family to be with you afterwards – people who understand the amount of work you have put into this research
Ensure that the timetable is clear	Ask previous students about their experience of the assessment process	Identify the questions that might be asked (especially any that you dread)	Be prepared to learn from any criticism or feedback	Thank your supervisors and any colleagues who have helped you
Make sure you have submitted the right documentation	Visit the room where it will take place in advance	Rehearse the process and reflect on it afterwards	Rehearse the process	Be prepared to help other students facing their assessment
	Rehearse the process with your supervisor or a group of students			

Using the framework to prepare yourself for the assessment

Finally, we need to focus on a holistic approach to getting ready for the assessment. This includes organising a mock *viva*, defence or presentation, but effective preparation for what can be a life-changing examination requires more than that. Table 11.4 demonstrates how we can use the five approaches to analyse the whole process.

In this chapter we have reviewed a range of rubrics that can be adapted for assessing research at various levels of the curriculum. We have looked at a system that could be used to help marking be more consistent and we have looked at various ways of preparing both the student and examiners for the assessment process. In the final chapter we look ahead to the future.

Chapter 12

Looking to the future

Where next?

In Chapter 1 we looked at some of the job roles that can appeal to postgraduates. In Chapter 6 we looked at transferable skills, how to identify the generic skills you have developed through doing research, and how to make them understandable to employers. In this final chapter there are two important issues to be covered: what makes research ethical, and therefore sustainable, and how you find and choose a job.

Ethics and the search for key values

If you want your research to stand the test of time and to help others by making a real contribution to the sum of all our knowledge, then it has to be good. Research that is based on falsified data, the result of coercion or other underhand tactics has no place in our world.

There are many instances where perpetrators of unethical practices have been exposed and paid dearly for them, often with much humiliation and the loss of a job. A German Minister of Defence, an eminent Dutch social psychologist and an American genetic research scientist are among them.

Finding some shared values that we can test dilemmas against so that we come up with the right (or best) answer has been a subject for the sociology of science for some time. Three types of tests have been suggested.

1 Testing for integrity: is the research reliable and free from fabrication, falsification or plagiarism?
2 Testing for protection of research subjects and practitioners
3 Testing for social responsibility.

Other values include communism (common ownership of intellectual property) and scientists being rewarded by recognition and esteem, universality (claims of truth based on impersonal criteria, not discriminatory by race, class, gender or nationality), organised scepticism (critical thinking, peer review) and selflessness (altruism). These have become known as CUDOS (Merton, 1942).

Some universities have tried to focus their thinking on the issues that most concern them. NTNU, a prestigious technical university in northern Norway, suggests that the following principles and practices should be focused on:

1 Transparency and confidentiality
2 Freedom of expression and loyalty
3 Acceptable and unacceptable relationships
4 Handling conflicts of interest
5 Blowing the whistle on dishonesty and research fraud
6 The research process: contracts and reporting routines
7 Governance of the relationship between the supervisor and the candidate/student
8 Storage, use and publication of data and personal data
9 Dilemmas of multidisciplinary work
10 Approvals and notification of research projects

(www.ntnu.edu/ethics-portal)

There are many guidelines about research ethics, national, international and discipline based. There are links to some of these at the end of the chapter.

Intellectual property

The question about who owns the data that is generated through research is an important one for supervisors to be clear about. In some cases an undergraduate and master's student might own their data, but the university might own the data collected and created by doctoral candidate. This can come as an unwelcome surprise to doctoral candidates. Some universities have a range of IP agreements with other businesses and employers if they co-sponsor research. These agreements might seek to prevent the publication of research for a period of time or limit the people who can be allowed work on particular projects. This is usually a matter of contract law, and the supervisor needs to know what rights and obligations they and their students have before they start the project. Chapter 8 in Taylor et al. (2018) has some useful information on this topic.

Ethics committees

Ethics committees have been established in most universities and within most national health services. Their first duty is the prevention of harm. Obtaining ethical approval for research projects has become a time-consuming and sometimes onerous task. Procedures that were invented to prevent harm during invasive clinical procedures on patients are sometimes applied to low-risk research on focus groups. However, even low-risk groups are entitled to participant information sheets, should sign documents demonstrating that they have understood the procedures and be guaranteed that their data will be anonymised, recorded accurately and kept secure. They have a right to know how the research has been funded and what will happen to the results of the study. Most researchers also have to say where participants can turn for support if they are upset or harmed by the procedures (see Wisker, 2012, p. 182 for more information). These are basic procedures which, now they have become mainstream, should take less time. Some research is more complex – if revealing the full purpose of the trial would mean that the resultant data might be compromised, then ethical approval to deceive is effectively being sought. These are the sorts of arguments that some chairs of ethics committees are better at managing than others, and it is the wise applicant who consults the committee informally to gain advice before finalising their application.

Some ethics committees now have recognised a pattern in low-risk research and can provide a pro forma (especially useful for undergraduate research), which if it is followed will normally be covered for ethical approval.

Whatever the research that needs to be carried out, gaining ethical approval does take time, often longer than could have been anticipated, and this needs to be factored into the timetable.

Career planning

This final part of the book is intended to help you to answer the following questions:

1   When in the research process should you start thinking about post-graduation career options?
2   In how many ways can you get help from your university in career planning?
3   How can you identify your own strengths, weaknesses, interests and options?
4   What sort of plan should you be putting together?

Supervisors are becoming more aware of the importance of a postgraduate student examining their career options early on in the research process. It is a good idea to seek an opening discussion in the first year. You need to think about possible career options early on so that you can work out how to use your research to support or widen those options.

The research you have carried out will be important in carrying you into your next job in at least three ways.

1   It demonstrates independence and problem-solving skills.
2   It opens the door for networking opportunities.
3   Your research is something that you can talk enthusiastically and knowledgably about at interviews (making it relevant to any interviewer).

There are several different ways you might approach thinking about your career. There are examples in Carter and Laurs (2014, p. 141, 145), from which some of the material in this section is drawn. We can look at these ways in terms of the five approaches to research supervision.

A list of possible occupations for PhD graduates

1   Research and development manager
2   Researcher
3   Function manager, i.e. working in functions such as marketing and production
4   Research policy and administration manager
5   Vocational or industrial trainer/instructor (including researcher developers and careers advisers/coaches)
6   IT and technology professional
7   Public/science engagement professional
8   Teaching professional
9   Journalist/editor

Other occupations reported by 3–4 per cent of respondents were: engineering professionals; health professionals; senior managers and officials; and management consultants and analysts (Haynes et al., 2016).

While most PhD graduates in Norway are employed, even there, there is still, as elsewhere, a problem with short-term contracts (Thun, Kyvik, Olsen, Vabo & Tomte, 2012).

Writing your CV

Work placements and shadowing are still excellent ways of finding out whether or not you are going to enjoy working in any particular environment. It is important to develop and use a wide network of contacts when seeking employment. Most careers advisors in universities will offer professional support in putting together job applications but in outline there are three types of CV from which you might want to choose.

*   *An academic CV* might include: education, awards, publications, conference papers and keynotes, projects, departmental activity, teaching, training and employment summary.
*   *A chronological CV* might include: education, employment, other activities (presentations, teaching and department activity), training and accreditation, referees.
*   *A competency-based CV* might include: personal profile, professional skills, education, employment, other activities, HE teaching and departmental activity, referees.

Table 12.1 Creating some career options

Functional	Enculturation	Critical thinking	Emancipation	Relationship development
Does your institution have a specialised postgraduate careers advisor?	Are there previous graduates who you can talk to about a range of careers options?	Look at local, national and international patterns. Where are the opportunities?	Audit your own interests, strengths and weaknesses by answering the following questions:	Look at the career paths of people you know and are working with. Ask them what made them make various decisions
What online career tools are available?	Be willing to meet people in your supervisor's network and start to create your own	Explore all options including: academic, academic-related, non-academic research posts, professional, charitable, business, public-service-related options	1 What are you good at? 2 What are your interests, motivations and values? 3 What do you most enjoy at university? 4 What kind of life-style do you want? 5 What do you want from your career?	Find a mentor to read your application forms and share their interview experiences with you
Are mock interviews available?	What work experience is available?	Collect a range of adverts and job descriptions to compare them with the answers to the self-audit questions	Identify the criteria that are important to you and complete a decision chart (Table 12.2)	

Longer-term trends

Trends in longer-term employment for doctoral graduates have been measured three years from graduation. This research highlighted the major value of doctoral study to researchers, employers and society. There was good evidence for the relative employability and value of doctoral graduates. It identified an earnings premium for those with a PhD over those with a master's degree but warned against the economic insecurity caused by short- and fixed-term post-doctoral contracts (Mellors-Bourne et al., 2013).

How to aim for an academic career

In Chapter 9 we explored how to get published. Along with developing a teaching portfolio, this is considered to be the first rung to be mastered on the ladder of an academic career. However, in many disciplines and in many countries, the opportunities for joining the professoriate are limited, albeit not impossible. You need to inform yourself realistically about the position you are facing if this is your aspiration. North America has more professors and more differentiated positions. In Germany, some parts of Switzerland and Poland, a professor with a full chair can be very powerful, whereas in the UK, Ireland and North America the departmental hierarchy makes for a flatter structure. France had a programme offering permanent positions to academics between 28 and 38 years. Several European countries require a *habilitation* (a post-doctoral qualification) before an academic can be considered for a professorial position. Aiming for an academic career in any country is likely to require persistence, but there will be more opportunities in some disciplines and some countries than in others (Else, 2015).

In the UK there is a concordat to support the career development of researchers. It has been signed by many funding bodies, universities, associations and government groups. Signatories support the recruitment and valuing of researchers and the promotion of diversity and equality, and promise to audit progress in strengthening the attractiveness and sustainability of research careers (Vitae, 2008).

The many books by Ron Barnett (2000, 2004, 2009, 2018) looking philosophically at the role of the university can be a useful window on the world. More practical is the advice from Shelda Debowski (2017). Her book is mostly about academic development, but she also covers the stages of the academic career cycle, different types of teaching and research-focused roles as well as programme management. The five approaches to supervising research can help us to untangle some opportunities here.

A role for the entrepreneurial researcher

The move to flatter organisations and portfolio careers has focused some universities to looking at encouraging entrepreneurialism. They have collaborated

Table 12.2 Aiming for an academic career

Functional	Enculturation	Critical thinking	Emancipation	Relationship development
Identify 'preparing to teach in HE' programmes and support attendance on them	Arrange for mentoring	Analyse the market for academic posts in your discipline over time. How mobile do others have to be to be successful in their field? What other attributes do successful academics have?	Investigate a wide range of possible institutions, roles within them, career paths and future research areas	Discuss career paths with supervisor and other academics
Find sample academic CVs and investigate a typical recruitment procedure	Encourage networking			Meet other friends and colleagues who are willing to advise you
	Support getting published early			
	Involve in grant applications			

with various institutions to establish business incubators (see for example the University of Bristol's 'SETsquared' partnership with local businesses and regional universities: www.bristol.ac.uk/business/resources-facilities/grow-business/).

Walsh, Hargreaves, Hillemann-Delaney and Li (2015) identified differing attitudes to the word 'entrepreneurship' between Chinese and British doctoral students working in STEM subjects. The Chinese students saw entrepreneurship as a more worthwhile endeavour, involving a positive attitude towards networking and creating diverse friendship groups, and linked to social as well as commercial development. The British doctoral candidates were more likely to have a negative attitude towards entrepreneurship and define it in terms of commercial gain. Nearly 80 per cent of their sample of Chinese doctoral students (n=114) expected to be involved in entrepreneurship activities in the future, compared with 28 per cent of the British candidates (n=146).

The authors were concerned that 'because some British researchers have a negative and unrealistic view of entrepreneurialism, they may miss or reject opportunities presented by entrepreneurial careers' (Walsh et al., p. 13). An additional concern was that a negative attitude towards the needs of commerce or industry might result in a reduction of government and/or industry funding for doctoral-level work.

This focus on entrepreneurialism is also reflected in the lens especially created by Vitae.ac.uk to explore the attributes gained by researchers that can be applied to the entrepreneurial worker. They call this the 'enterprise lens' (see Figure 12.1). It emphasises such attributes as the ability to sustain relationships with stakeholders, supporting knowledge transfer, knowledge of the principles behind intellectual property, financial management and resilience.

You may you find that you have two decision points when planning your career.

- Stage One: what type of career do you want in what type of organisation? To answer that question you can use your research skills to populate a slightly amended version of the decision table below (Table 12.3). The headings across the top might read: international business, tertiary education, public service, university, research institute, self-employment. Then you would have a list of possible employers and can start the second stage of listing your criteria down the left-hand side of the page.
- Stage Two: having identified possible employers you will be seeking job opportunities with several of them, and then (hopefully) be in a position to choose between two or more opportunities. A second decision-taking chart will help you to analyse the situation. Some people jump straight to Stage Two because they already have a vocation or know environmentally exactly how or where they want to spend their lives.

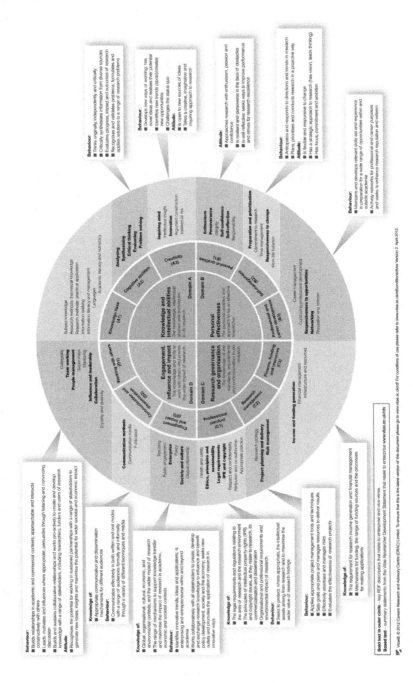

Figure 12.1 Enterprise lens on the Vitae Researcher Development Framework

Table 12.3 A draft decision-making table for choosing between job opportunities

	Job A	Job B	Job C	Job D
Level of interest in the work itself				
Future opportunities				
Good colleagues to work with				
Sufficient remuneration				
Location				
Organisation that has values I agree with				
Others				
Simple total score or ranked score according to importance of each item				

Creating a decision-taking chart

When you have identified a range of options, you can make a decision by identifying your key criteria and ranking each job opportunity against these criteria. You could give each option a score out of ten – just add up the columns and take the highest score. However, completing the table is likely to make you debate the criteria more finely, and therefore you may come to a more nuanced conclusion. Either way, the table will have done its job. A sample is shown below.

As we saw in Chapter 6, the skills agenda has now largely been accepted as an important development. The formation of a professional body across Europe: Professionals in Doctoral Education (PRIDE) (www.pride-prsoject.eu /Home/) demonstrates again the importance of this new cadre of people engaged in various aspects of generic skills training.

Beyond the next job

We are also educating our postgraduate researchers to be leaders in a global and mobile world. The majority of them do not continue as academic researchers: some move into education as teachers or academics and 50 per cent move into other public services or business (Ball, Metcalf, Pearce & Shinton, 2009). In these fast-moving times I have suggested that we need to be much more ambitious for our graduates and postgraduates.

The thesis of this book is that we need to focus on how we educate the globally competent graduate or postgraduate researcher. Some of the skills you will learn are already familiar in outline: the ability to design research projects, skills of analysis and academic writing, the ability to find, assimilate and synthesise large amounts of information on any given subject, the ability to manage a project ethically and present findings intelligibly. These are the given skills that we expect every student to have. I suggest you need a broader base and a higher aspiration.

Our postgraduate students need to understand the philosophy of knowledge, as it is interpreted in their discipline and in others; they need to understand how that knowledge will be created and used in different societies, the sociology and politics of knowledge creation.

Students who are engaged in cross-disciplinary research can have real problems if confronted by academics who are used to one way of thinking and one recommended approach to conducting the research. They need to be able to anticipate, analyse and make reasoned judgements about the disciplinary and ethical issues that are going to arise in the work that they seek to do. Arguably, every postgraduate student needs a grounding in law so that you can understand contracts in different countries and how intellectual property is viewed.

It is our research-competent postgraduates who, I think, will form the pool of people from whom our future leaders will be drawn. Therefore, it becomes important to develop a strategic vision, to anticipate at least some of the effects of your research and learn how to influence governments, businesses and the voluntary sector. For example, the leading engineer needs to confront the ethical question of how their work might be used, and if their research creates environmental damage they might feel obliged to move into the interdisciplinary area of life-cycle analysis and environmental research. They also need to be looking to their future and asking how they can build capacity to continue the important research that they have begun.

In some cases this aspirational list of leadership roles favours the multilingual, high-flying generalist more than the bench researcher who just wants to work in a laboratory or at a computer. While we need brilliant minds that can do brilliant research, we also need brilliant people to apply and develop that work – which is where the hitherto frequently undervalued professional doctorates might come in. We might well ask, alongside a recent workshop on the future of doctoral education, is 'transnational research' the new 'transnational education'? We started this book with the question 'is it worth it?' There is an opportunity cost to undertaking education, but wisely applied with open eyes to the future, undertaking a substantial research project is certainly a rare opportunity to become expert in a field. To develop the highest skills in problem solving, to learn how to start into something completely new and to work with colleagues from around the world are skills that society needs. If you can use all these skills to make the whole process 'worth it' you will have a very useful and absorbing life ahead.

Websites for further research on ethical issues

International protocols

Allea European code of conduct for research integrity (revised ed.). www.allea.org/wp-content/uploads/2017/03/ALLEA-European-Code-of-Conduct-for-Research-Integrity-2017-1.pdf

Montreal statement on research integrity in cross-boundary research collaborations. www.researchintegrity.org/Statements/Montreal%20Statement%20English.pdf

Singapore statement on research integrity. www.singaporestatement.org/

Concordat to support research integrity. www.universitiesuk.ac.uk/highereducation/Documents/2012/TheConcordatToSupportResearchIntegrity.pdf

Vancouver rules on publication. www.icmje.org/icmje-recommendations.pdf

The ten focus points (NTNU Norway). www.ntnu.edu/ethics-portal

Research ethics in Sweden

www.eurecnet.org/information/sweden.html

Codex: rules and guidelines for research. www.codex.vr.se/en/index.shtml

Research ethics committees in Norway

National Committee for Research Ethics in the Social Sciences and the Humanities (NESH), Norwegian National Research Ethics Committee for Medical and Health Research (NEM), National Committee for Research Ethics in Science and Technology (NENT). Covering medical and health research; science and technology; social sciences, law and the humanities; human remains; internet research. www.etikkom.no/en/our-work/about-us/the-national-commission-for-the-investigation-of-research-misconduct/

Further resources on careers

Careers in research: www.rcuk.ac.uk/skills/percase/booklets/(booklets on careers in: history, social science, physics, engineering, environment, biology and chemistry)

Career stories on film: www.vitae.ac.uk/researcher-careers/researcher-career-stories/list-of-vitae-career-stories-on-film/vitae-career-stories-on-film-list (stories from people who completed doctorates in art, computer science, molecular pathology, high energy physics, marketing, geology, chemistry, information science, metallurgy, biology/life sciences, plant ecophysiology, artificial intelligence, glaciology, engineering geology, music and psychology. Variously they went on to follow careers in composing, research for commercial and non-commercial organisations, entrepreneurship, academia, financial advising, business operations, educational research, research translation, intellectual property, medicine, educational development and pottery).

Appendix A

Theoretical background: emergence of the framework

An introduction to the theories behind the framework

In Chapter 2 we saw a brief outline of the framework itself. Here I want to explain more about the theoretical background to each of the approaches, and at is at this point that many advanced students begin to really understand why it can work for them.

There are different core values behind each of the approaches. So the core value behind the functional approach is *performativity*: the desire and expectation that there will be targets and goals, a timetable, measurable outputs, a programme and a plan. The advantage of these clear signposts is that it is quite obvious whether or not a piece of work is 'on track' –well, in one way, but as we see later, there are other measures of quality that we need to take into account. However, as an approach it has an important place in our lexicon. The disciplines that inform this approach are more about organisational development, business management, accounting and some branches of economics. To identify whether or not a statement or action falls under this approach we would look to see if it was related towards achieving tangible objectives.

The core value behind enculturation is *belonging*. For students and supervisors who prize this approach there is a strong sense of direction, of being part of a group. The theoretical bases are sociology and epistemology. To identify whether or not a statement or action falls under this approach we would look to see if its intention was to include someone.

The core value behind critical thinking is *rigour*. It is more than 'does this piece of work fit into the discipline?', it is 'will this piece of work withstand an attack by any discipline?' Is it philosophically and scientifically sound or are there unrecognised flaws in the argumentation? To identify whether or not a statement or action falls under this approach we would look to see if its intention was to critically analyse and evaluate.

The core value behind emancipation is *autonomy*. Here, success is measured not by external objectives but by personal growth. Self-actualisation is often described as the goal and the theoretical base comes from humanistic psychology. To identify whether or not a statement or action falls under this approach we would look to see if its intention was to develop others. So under critical thinking it is the argument that is most important, under emancipation it is the development of the independent person.

The core value behind relationship development is *love*. Love in the sense of 'agape' (from the Greek: an altruistic benevolence). Friendship and empathy are important virtues and the theoretical understanding would come from work around social psychology and some branches of virtue ethics. To identify whether or not a statement or action falls under this approach we would look to see if it was truly altruistic. Table A1 summarises these key elements of the approaches to research supervision.

Alternative models for exploring the role of supervisor and needs of the student

There are now a range of models for looking at research supervision. Gatfield (2005) based his research on the Blake and Mouton managerial grid model, and verified his work through 12 in-depth interviews with supervisors. He found two axes of 'support' and 'structure' and argued that where support and structure are low the academics' style was found to be laissez-faire, and where support and structure were high, there was a contractual style. A pastoral style would mean that the academic provided high personal support but left the student to manage the structure of their research project, and the directorial style would do the reverse. Gatfield argues (as I do) that no one approach is right.

From this much simplified summary of Gatfield's work we can see that it does not explicitly address the issue of critical thinking. It is also doubtful whether we can superimpose the other terms directly on the framework, for example the terms such as 'low structure' and 'emancipatory' are not really the same.

Murphy, Bain and Conrad (2007) produced another four-quadrant matrix from interviews with 17 engineering supervisors and their students (34 participants in total), which looked at guiding and controlling on one axis and person and task focus on the other. Murphy and her colleagues also make the observation that supervision models are linked to beliefs about teaching, and this view is backed up by the research for this book.

Murphy usefully creates detailed descriptions of each of the quadrants that her model creates. She analyses them along with many factors including the role of the supervisor, the role of the candidate, outcomes, decision making and focus. Again, if we plot the framework in this book against the axis proposed by Murphy et al. (see Figure 13.1) we see some of the differences – in Murphy's model there is potentially a conflation of two elements: functional and critical thinking.

In this instance the conflation is between a core task of supervision (developing critical thinking) and the functional task of the institution (achieving completion on time within quality assurance measures). Similar reservations

Table A1 Some core values and the theoretical background to the framework

	Functional	Enculturation	Critical thinking	Emancipation	Relationship development
Core values	Performativity	Belonging	Rigour	Autonomy	Love Agape
What people might be seeking	Certainty Clear signposts Evidence of progress	Belonging A sense of direction Direction towards career openings Role models	Opportunities to think in new ways Ability to analyse and recognise flaws in arguments	Opportunity to set own direction and discover a personally meaningful framework Self-actualisation	Friendship Empathy
Theoretical bases	Organisational development Economics	Sociology Epistemology	Philosophy Scientific logic	Humanistic psychology	Social psychology Virtues
Identified by the intent to	Achieve objectives	Include	Analyse	Develop others	Be altruistic

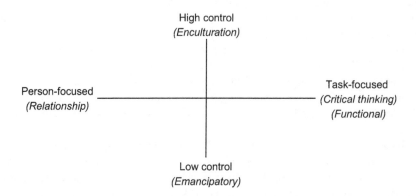

High control
(Enculturation)

Person-focused
(Relationship)

Task-focused
(Critical thinking)
(Functional)

Low control
(Emancipatory)

Figure A1 An interpretation of Murphy et al.'s model contrasted with the five approaches

to those expressed in the comparison with the Gatfield model remain about aligning the terms 'low control' and 'emancipatory' and 'high control' and 'enculturation'.

These two models provide a useful contrast to the framework proposed in this book, but a four-quadrant matrix is more limiting in terms of analysis. The framework proposed here is multi-dimensional: it has five approaches analysed in a large number of ways (e.g. values, independency to dependency, developing creativity, lecturing and curriculum design). The proposal that I am making here is that as many elements as possible should become transparent to both the academic and the postgraduate student.

A second, frequently described approach was created originally by Acker, who looked at the 'technical rational model' (where the goal is either the creation of an independent researcher, scholarly creativity or speedy completion) and contrasted it with the 'negotiated order model' where there are 'many unspoken agendas operating throughout the research process and mutual expectations are subject to negotiation and change over time' (Acker, Hill & Black, 1994). This approach problematises supervision and links to the functional approach described later in this book.

Grant and others have used a small number of cases of master's and doctoral supervision, analysed the dialogue and described the power dynamic of the Hegelian 'master–slave' or 'apprenticeship' models (Grant, 2005, 2008). A development of this approach moves the focus away from the supervisor–student dyad and looks at the practices implied by the model of 'communities of practice' (Lave & Wenger, 1991) – this is, in effect, offering a decentralised version of the master–apprentice role. Lave and Wenger's work has had great impact in highlighting sociological issues implicit in teaching and learning, and they explore the way in which the student is helped (or not) to move through legitimate peripheral participation to an understanding and mastery of the tacit knowledge required to participate fully in an academic community. This element is explored further in the 'enculturation' approach to teaching and supervision (see Chapter 4).

Lovitts argues that the components needed for creative work are: domain-relevant skills (intelligence and knowledge), creativity (thinking styles and personality) and task motivation. She also identifies the micro and macro environments that the student is operating in, and argues that the micro environment (in particular the relationship between student and their advisor) is the most important (Lovitts, 2007).

Halse and Malfroy (2010) have retheorised doctoral supervision as professional work and linked it conceptually with Aristotle's intellectual virtues. They include *phronesis* (habits of the mind), which is a combination of critical thinking and engagement; *episteme* (theoretical knowledge acquired through reflection and thinking) by which they mean fruitful participation in scholarly expertise by producing articles and scholarly papers; and *techne*, which relates to the capacity to write and communicate, use scientific resources, manage information and time. They also refer to the obligations of the learning alliance (the agreement between the student and supervisor) which has links to some informal contracts that might be made between supervisor and student about such issues as the kind of feedback that a student is willing and able to accept and give (robust, honest, gentle?).

The research for this book

Methods and samples

A variety of methods have been used to explore both the generalisability of the proposed framework and the acceptability, range and depth of information that each method produced. Some of the methods came from traditional qualitative research methods. The original interviews with academics took place in a research-led university in the UK, and subsequent interviews took place with academics at Harvard University, USA and at other research-led universities in the UK. In addition an experiential element has been added: many workshops have taken place in Sweden, Estonia, Denmark and the UK between 2007 and 2011. Interviews and focus groups with students took place over the same period. The poster session also took place during a teaching and learning conference in 2008. The study was given approval by the UK university's ethics committee and was conducted in accordance with the British Psychological Society's Code of Practice.

One significant difference between this book and the work of many other authors is that there was a balance of interviewees between scientific and social science disciplines. Others have concentrated more on arts and social science disciplines (for example, Grant, 2005; Wisker, 2012; Hockey, 1994, 1996).

Stage 1: qualitative interviews

The framework was first created from an analysis of interviews with 12 UK academics and focus groups with 20 students (not necessarily from the same pairs). The sample of academics was purposive: excellent supervisors from across a range of disciplines were interviewed. There were four female and eight male academics. The sample of students was opportunistic, but included master's and doctoral students from soft and hard applied subjects and soft pure subject groups.

The framework was extended and deepened with further interviews: three supervisors at Harvard (they call them 'advisors') were all male and came from pure hard and applied disciplines. Subsequent interviews have taken place in the UK with more female academics and those working in the humanities and arts to balance the sample. A few core questions were asked of each interviewee in semi-structured interviews, and then there were follow-up probes and a section of questions theorising with the interviewee (Cousin, 2009).

The probes included checking for salience by asking if the respondent felt a point was a widely held view, and some hypothetical questions relating discipline to pedagogy. Hesitations and ambiguities were followed up and each interviewee had a copy of their transcript to check before it was analysed.

Focus groups and interviews have been held with postgraduate students and analysed in a similar manner. Participants in conference discussions, at workshops on teaching and learning and on supervision development programmes have also contributed enormously to the evolution of this book.

All the academics interviewed were recommended as 'excellent' either by colleagues or by students, and sometimes by both. The interviews were all recorded and transcribed. The transcripts were initially coded and analysed into themes while looking for underlying concepts. Eventually, the data settled into five areas which were united by an over-arching tension for the academics between the professional and the personal self.

The transcripts were then coded in several ways. Initially, themes were created from the data (which led to the framework), and then statements were abstracted in relationship to certain questions (such as 'independence' and 'creativity') and compared with each other.

Stage 2: questionnaires

Workshops with academics were held in five research-led universities in the UK and Scandinavia, where the participants were asked to rate each approach on a Likert scale for:

- importance to their practice (salience)
- how much they used an approach in their practice (espoused theory and theory-in-use, Argyris and Schon, 1974)

- how much they would like to be skilled in a particular approach (development opportunities).

Fifty-five questionnaires were analysed. Confidentiality and anonymity were assured. These questionnaires were designed to enable comparison of approach to supervision by discipline.

To assess whether the data is internally consistent as a whole and whether each approach is also internally consistent, it was entered into SPSS, and the Cronbach's alpha reliability score over 15 items was 0.775. Cronbach's alpha was also run for each approach and four out of five of them were acceptable.

The functional items scored 0.156. This is a very low score for reliability and may be explained by the fact that the functional approach is seen by some as a management or political tool, so for example, they may use this approach but not value it (an observation borne out by reactions in several of the workshops exploring this framework). The other Cronbach's alpha scores were: enculturation 0.717; critical thinking 0.547; emancipation 0.833 and quality of relationship 0.685.

Small sample numbers meant that we cannot generalise about disciplinary differences, but if the results were replicated on a larger sample we could suggest that (after a workshop) supervisors can differentiate between the approaches and those from the hard pure subject groups might respond more readily to development opportunities that emphasised a critical thinking, enculturation and quality of relationship approaches.

Stage 3: interactive poster session

An opportunistic sample of 35 academics was invited to see if there is any relationship between discipline, conceptions of knowledge and approaches to supervision. The academics were attending a teaching and learning event and were asked to volunteer to identify their discipline in terms of hard, soft, pure and applied (see below). They then identified their preferred approaches to supervision by using different coloured stickers on posters. This was a public act and we would need further investigation to check whether that distorted the findings. There was an opportunity for academics to contribute new and different perceptions outside those proposed by Biglan (1973a, 1973b) and from the original research.

Two of the academics found it difficult to identify their discipline in Biglan's terms. However, they did accept that their work spanned two of the categories and were content to participate providing their contributions could be 'double-counted'.

Stage 4: workshops

Workshops were held for groups of between 10 and 60 academics at research-led universities in the UK, Sweden, Denmark, Estonia and at European and international conferences, where groups of academics have used this framework to explore how to resolve research, supervision and teaching dilemmas. Subsequent interviews and correspondence with some of these academics demonstrate that using the framework in this way can have a powerful illuminative effect and give the academic much greater self-confidence in their ability to resolve some of these dilemmas. The dilemmas that are discussed in these sessions are typically those addressed in Chapter 10.

To look for disciplinary differences, I adapted the two-dimensional model of subject characteristics proposed by Biglan (see Table A2) and discussed by Becher and Trowler (2001). Some subjects are in transition across disciplinary boundaries and 'double counting' was used to reflect this.

Table A2 has been adapted because some subjects have changed their emphasis, for example economics has become increasingly mathematical and so econometrics has been included in the 'hard applied' category.

In the supervisor's edition of this book all the quotes from supervisors in this text were allocated to one of these quadrants to preserve their anonymity and to enable comparison across disciplines. One of the themes that emerged from this analysis is that there is less difference between the disciplines when we examine research supervision than is suggested by previous authors who have examined pedagogies in the disciplines (Becher & Trowler, 1989). The supervisors interviewed for this work gave clear examples of a functional approach regardless of whether they were engineers or educationalists. Both they and the philosophers and pure scientists could all give examples of each

Table A2 The relationships between subject matter characteristics and the structure and output of university departments (adapted from Biglan 1973a, 1973b)

	HARD *Similar paradigm for content and research methods. More co-authors, more influences on research. Subjects more physical. Reality is more objective.*	**SOFT** *Similar paradigm for content and research methods. Research more independent. Subjects more relative/relational. Reality is more subjective.*
PURE	Biochemistry, Botany, Chemistry, Maths, Microbiology, Physics, Physiology	Dance, English, Languages, Linguistics, Political science, Philosophy, Psychology, Sociology, Theology, Translation, Music
APPLIED *More time spent on service activities*	Econometrics, Engineering (inc. Chemical, Civil, Structural, Electronic, Materials etc.), Computer science, Environmental science, Food and nutrition, Medicine, Space technology	Business Studies, Accounting, Finance, Economics, Education, Educational development Law, Management (inc. Tourism, Retail and Hospitality), Nursing and health care

approach. No one supervisor gave examples of every approach but when we took all the interviews together, each disciplinary group did.

More recent research relating to the five approaches

From Australia

An investigation has been carried out in Australia where a team of psychologists from Australia National University used the innovative Choice-Based Conjoint (CBC) methodology to investigate the importance of different supervisory functions to Australian postgraduate students. There were 14 students studying at either master's or doctoral levels and they came from a range of disciplines including seven from psychology and others from international relations, archaeology, medicine, economics, history and anthropology. Their results suggested that students preferred supervisors who fostered caring/supportive relationships over those who focused more strictly on instrumental functions (Roach, Rieger & Christensen, in press).

Their analysis suggested that the students surveyed ranked critical thinking and enculturation as their first priority, the second priority was relationship and emancipation, and the functional approach was least prioritised. There were no differences in preference between male and female students, over age or length of study. However, there is a suggestion that students from the faculty of arts and education prioritised enculturation and relationships more than students from the faculty of science and technology. This is not a surprising finding given that many students in arts and education work more in isolation whereas students in science and technology tend to work as members of a laboratory team. It suggests that students doing research in arts and education need to pay more attention to getting involved in the work of the department and creating a supportive network (the enculturation and relationships approaches) to compensate for this.

From Norway

Shalfawi carried out another investigation of PhD students' preferences for approaches as part of an assignment for a development programme for academics at the University of Stavanger in 2016. Shalfawi's sample was 59 students (total contacted were 282 = response rate of 21 per cent). The responses were subjected to a number of statistical tests and this next section quotes from his assignment (with his permission).

> The sample was first assessed using the Shapiro-Wilk test and Kolmogorov-Smirnov test (none of the answers were normally distributed ($P < 0.05$)). The accepted index for the current study on the Kaiser-Meyer-Olkin test was set to > 0.6. The Bartlett's test of Sphericity was assessed to

measure the validity and suitability of the responses collected through the study and the acceptance of Bartlett's test of Sphericity was set to P < 0.05. Thereafter the internal consistency was reported by Cronbach's a coefficient for the questionnaire and the sub-categories measured. Then Kruscal-Wallis test followed by Dunn's multiple comparisons test were performed to examine the order of the PhD student's supervising priorities and to investigate differences between male and female students' preferences. In order to determine the size of the difference, the effect size (Cohen's d) was calculated and considered small at (d = 0.2), moderate (d = 0.5) and large (d = 0.8) (Cohen 1988). Differences were considered significant at P # 0.05 and the results were expressed as means, standard deviations and rank sum difference.

Examination of internal consistency shows a KMO index of 0.69 and a statistical significant Bartlett's test of Sphericity (p < 0.001). Therefore and generally, the results of the present study support the requirements of good internal consistency and strengthen the conceptual approaches to supervision questionnaire as an effective means of measuring and identifying the conceptual approaches to supervision.

Shalfawi's further tests recommended adjusting item 2 under enculturation, item 4 under emancipation and item 10 under relationships to increase the validity and internal consistency of the responses. As a result of Shalfawi's work the questionnaires has been adapted further. He has subsequently carried out further tests and is clear that further validation is required.

A project by a group of three Norwegian universities led by Tor-Ivan Kaarlseen has looked at the results of a survey of 89 supervisors. This found no significant differences in approach by supervisors from different disciplines but there was a correlation between the more experienced supervisors and the relationship development approach (see the companion book also published by Routledge, *Successful Research Supervision* (Lee, 2019), Appendix A). We recognise that to validate these questionnaire properly we will need to substantially increase the number of questions and the response rate. It is planned to set the survey up online and readers are welcome to contact me at drannemllee@gmail.com if they are interested in participating in a much more extended study.

From the UK

In addition to Shalfawi's work, nearly 100 students completed a shorter online version of the questionnaire and over 80 students have completed the full questionnaire in various workshops. This is an ongoing project and we would welcome postgraduate students completing the online survey – please contact me for further details.

From the European Union and the USA

As a result of being involved in an Erasmus project on the modern doctorate (Fillery-Travis et al., 2017; Lee, 2018a), I was able to analyse fresh interview data arising from interviews with academics across the UK, Italy, the Netherlands and Eire. Transcripts of interviews with 40 more academics were analysed in detail and it was possible to allocate most of the transcripts among the five approaches. There was also a survey of 270 candidates and 124 supervisors (called 'advisors' in the US) who replied to a questionnaire from across Europe and the USA. This survey showed that both candidates and supervisors could distinguish between the five approaches and prioritise them. It contributed a considerable amount of qualitative information through answers to the open-ended questions. Interestingly, this group of candidates prioritised their academic supervisor's functional skills (the approach rated as the lowest priority by the previous two pieces of research with mostly full-time traditional doctoral students). In the Erasmus group there were more mature part-time professional students. Students had a more evenly spread expectation of their workplace advisors across the five approaches and the academic supervisors thought their highest priority was to offer critical thinking.

These generalisations might show that there are some differences among different groups in their expectations, but more importantly they show the need for individual supervisors and candidates to understand and articulate their strengths, needs and expectations both at an early stage in the relationship and as it evolves.

The researcher's background

No qualitative study should ignore the researcher's background, and some readers might want to know that I have a background in psychology but have also always had an interest in economics. I see the social–psychological and economic factors as key drivers in our economy. Professionally, I have worked in a range of public and private sector organisations, been a head teacher and run my own consultancy, before moving into academia. My own PhD was undertaken in a Department of Educational Studies, but looked at conflict around medical doctors in general practice, and included a wonderfully eclectic research methods programme. I had a new supervisor allocated to me halfway through my research, so I have sympathy with that predicament, and I had a wonderful peer group of research students to work with. I have an equal passion for research and for teaching and most (but not all) of my postgraduate students have been very successful. My regret has always been that I did not study philosophy as an undergraduate, and this may explain why the strand 'critical thinking' has been of great interest to me.

Some readers might want to know if this framework flows from a cognitive or phenomenographic perspective (Ackerlind, 2008). Ackerlind argues that two key perspectives are the cognitive constructivist where the objective is conceptual change and it is assumed that different conceptions are independent of each other, whereas the phenomenographic constitutionalist perspective sees different conceptions related in a hierarchy of inclusiveness and its objective is conceptual expansion. I argue that this framework facilitates a growing awareness of the range of approaches that the academic can take to supporting the student doing research. Perhaps its strength is that it enables aspects of both perspectives to be used, for example the academic can use it to *compare and contrast* their approaches and *expand* awareness of the range of approaches available.

Using the framework to support compare and contrast, and expanding awareness.

A typical workshop for postgraduate students using this framework might ask the participant to:

1   Reflect (in an anonymous pre-workshop survey) on their priorities and how they perceive the strengths and weaknesses of their supervisors
2   Identify their own strengths in doing research and compare these with other colleagues
3   Examine how many long-term career options the student wants to keep open and how their current research project can be used to help them
4   Explore the practical steps that a student can take to find the support they need
5   Analyse and evaluate the power of various milestones
6   Critically investigate the 'habitas' that the student will be engaged with
7   Describe how their relationship with their supervisor begins, develops over time and their reaction to the different stages.

The research behind this book could be described as positivist because it does create a framework. As we have seen it is not the only framework possible and the boundaries are permeable, but many have found it useful when analysing their own practice and when trying to increase the options they have when confronted by perplexing situations with students.

There is a political undercurrent to this book; the increasing pressure to have larger numbers of students at postgraduate level and for research students to complete their studies within a limited time is encouraging performativity, compliance with institutional norms and instrumentality. I believe that an over-emphasis on the functional approach, to the exclusion of all others, creates a rigid and arid experience for both academic and student, so the introduction of four other approaches to working with research students is a deliberate attempt to put the functional approach in its rightful place. New academics need to master the functional skills, and this book does encourage that because if they do not they may never feel comfortable using the other approaches. But after that they need to be encouraged to look at how they teach and the core values they are espousing in a more critical manner.

In this chapter I have described the theoretical background to the five approaches and reviewed some of the alternative models that have been provided for looking at research supervision – most of them focusing on doctoral supervision. I have made the research behind this framework as clear as possible – it used a multi-method but largely qualitative approach, and included some less usual, but illuminating, ways of testing the data.

Appendix B
A summary of key practices in the disciplines abstracted from the Carnegie Initiative on the Doctorate (Golde & Walker, 2006)

Sciences

Doctoral students working in the sciences are not usually as lonely as some in the humanities or social sciences can be. Scientists usually work long hours in laboratory teams. The doctoral student may learn as much from a neighbouring post-doctoral student as from their supervisor.

The Carnegie Initiative on the Doctorate (CID) project recommended that the contradictions and inconsistencies of science must be cherished; scientists must be able to take risks but also be rigorous in their work and conscious of the public context. The single most important issue is choosing and defining a problem and locating it in a larger map of the field, and this needs reassessing every two years. The approximate degree of intellectual security must be articulated. 'On-going critical reflection in the form of a departmental seminar on the state of knowledge in the discipline must be an integral part of doctoral training' (Elkana, 2006, p. 72). A critical study of selected biographies of past caretakers of the profession should be pursued. Scientific knowledge is not always cumulative; when what has gone before is disproved it is frequently omitted from future teaching (unless it forms a lesson in how not to do something).

Mathematics

Mathematics is an international discipline. Its language is readily understood by all mathematicians, but in the past mathematicians have often divided themselves into two groups: pure and applied. They also frequently work on their own.

Algebra, number theory, probability, analysis, logic, differential equations, geometry and topology form part of pure maths, which is akin to an art. Applied maths is pure maths applied to problems. Some mathematicians argue that this barrier is artificial and should be dropped. There is concern about the decline in interest in maths from Western students and two suggestions for over-coming this are: first, to encourage team rather than the individual working which has become the norm; and second, to encourage ownership of problems by the students creating them, rather than supervisors allocating the next problem in their research programme to the next doctoral student. If pure and applied maths are to merge, the requirement for mathematicians to be able to work with multi-disciplinary teams will increase.

Mathematical knowledge tends to be cumulative, unlike sciences; new maths builds on but does not discard what has come before.

Chemistry

Doctoral students may join a lab and work for some months before they are allocated a supervisor. There are many 'grand challenges' which need the chemist's skills (for example, to develop unlimited and inexpensive energy, with new ways of energy generation, storage and transportation), but there can be problems of over-specialisation and the atomistic nature of the subject can limit doctoral students' awareness of interdisciplinary matters. The two basic aspects of a chemist's work are substances and transformation, but the 'grand challenges' mean that interdisciplinary research is vital. Chemists, too, must now be ready to work in multi-disciplinary teams.

A useful suggestion from this discipline is that doctoral students can be usefully charged with the responsibility of inviting outside specialists for departmental colloquia.

Compared with many other fields, chemistry has far to go in achieving gender, age and racial diversity. The typical doctoral student is a white male of 28 years. The career expectation is of a life working at the bench, yet in practice this does not always happen. If chemistry is to remain a central discipline it is necessary to prepare chemists for a life where they will also need more generic skills.

Neuroscience

This is the study of brain and brain function, and is an example of a relatively new field that embraces pharmacology, psychology, biology, biomedical sciences, nanotechnology, bioengineering, mathematics, chemistry, computing and even some sociology. Neuroscience doctoral students, therefore, will come from one disciplinary background, and will have to understand others before they can pursue their research. The challenge for neuroscience then, is to manage boundaries productively while retaining its core expertise. This conflict between breadth and depth can be solved to some extent by generalised training programmes to extend students' existing knowledge and laboratory rotations. The challenge is to maintain quality within this explosion of knowledge. Other disciplines define their unit of analysis automatically (e.g. molecular biology, cell biology). The challenge for neuroscience is to bring together a top-down and a bottom-up approach in a rigorous manner. A neuroscientist needs to be aware of the trajectory of work in all adjacent disciplines; Hymen calls this a 'Janus-like' quality. One test of competence in the discipline is a pragmatic one: can a doctoral student read and criticise any paper in the field's general journals?

The journal club has been identified as a signature pedagogy for neuroscience and customary in most biological science departments. A single article is usually presented by a member of the department; participation including doctoral students, post-doctoral researchers and academic faculty is expected. Journal clubs teach critical analysis, presenting skills and (because they are often inter-departmental) encourage interdisciplinarity. This practice effectively consolidates knowledge in a fast-moving field. Many humanities and education journals publish four or six editions a year, yet one immunology journal publishes 52 editions a year.

Education

If neuroscience is an example of how disciplinary boundaries are falling, educa-tion is an example of how one discipline can permeate every other one. Every discipline is concerned about how it is taught, so disciplinary pedagogy is of interest to all. Education also requires an ability to understand politics, psych-ology, sociology, philosophy, learning theories, administration, management and economics. This broad base has led critics to perceive a lack of quality in educa-tional research but leads us to understand that doctoral students in education need not only to ensure scholarly rigour, but they also need to be able to defend their paradigm to all-comers.

Everyone in the academic world has been a student at some point. Many EdD students have also been teachers and doctoral students are likely to be mature entrants who begin their studies with strong beliefs about the nature of teaching and learning. This provides fertile soil for reflection, which should extend every student's methodological understanding. Proof in education is a very elusive characteristic, it is not much of an experimental science (although there is a significant role for pilot studies) yet educationalists need to be able to speak persuasively of qualitative matters to quantitative scientists.

History

Historians can be either social science or humanities based. The notion of cul-tural capital is an example of a topic which moves across boundaries. History has moved to take into account different perspectives (for example from a Western perspective to a global one); historians are creating a well-grounded narrative, but, like scientists, they have to recognise that new discoveries may make their 'knowledge' instantly redundant. These narratives are based on primary sources – documents are a vital tool of the trade. The regular seminar is a major method of teaching, where arguments will be presented in front of other students, tested and challenged.

Skills of classifying, decoding, comparing, contextualising and communicating explain why many historians undertake careers outside academia. They have to anyway, because these days there are far fewer posts for them.

English

There is a basic division in the subject between literature and composition. In English there is a recognised (if disputed) canon. This canon can be broken down into a List. The List is a group of works that forms the basis of study for a particular programme and it might comprise 60 or 100 works. At a doctoral level the student and supervisor might work together to create an acceptable list which will reflect the student's position (for example, Romanticism or feminism in a certain period). Mastering this list can take many solitary months.

There are some fundamental questions in English: what is national literature? What counts as the best writing? Are there better or worse ways of reading texts? What is the relationship between literature and its media? There has long been a tradition of understanding that teaching a subject encourages mastery of it, and this opportunity occurs frequently for English doctoral students in the USA.

The CID project detected strong gender issues in the study of English. They argued that in the USA the subject is becoming feminised with increasing numbers of female undergraduate students, but that there is still a legacy of patronising paternalism in the hierarchy. While that paternalism may or may not be gender biased, they quote a fascinating unsent letter from an English student to her professor:

> 'Too bad' she says 'I am leaving this course feeling just as separate from, intimidated by, in awe of, and ultimately uninterested in (the great texts we were being introduced to) as I was when I entered. Sometimes I wonder if that's what you actually want – to keep us from joining some charmed inner circle of knowledge'.
>
> (Abernethy, 2006, p. 358)

Joining this charmed inner circle of knowledge is exactly what we *are* aiming to do when we use a 'communities of practice' approach to creating stewards of the discipline.

From this brief summary of some of the characteristics or ambitions of the doctoral process in different disciplines, we can see some interesting ideas emerging which could be used by other disciplines or which could become more applicable as disciplinary boundaries fade.

Appendix C

Critical thinking: key terms used in research

Use this list to identify which terms are central to your work and explore others to broaden your understanding of different approaches to research

Key terms to be explored	15 Epistemological frameworks
1 Abductive	16 Ethnography
2 Action research	17 Event driven (vs time driven)
3 Alternatives	18 Experiment
4 Axiomatic logic	19 Explaining transitions
5 Canon	20 Explanation
6 Causation	21 Field work
7 Chronological	22 Generalisability
8 Comparison	23 Generating theory
9 Constructivism	24 Hermeneutics
10 Contributing to theory	25 Hypothesis testing
11 Critical realism	26 Inductive
12 Deductive	27 Interpretation
13 Description	28 Intersubjectivity
14 Empirical	29 Interviews

30 Logical consistency	43 Qualitative
31 Measurement	44 Quantitative
32 Meta analysis	45 Reflexivity
33 Narrative and stories	46 Reproducibility/repeatability
34 Observation	47 Retroductive
35 Paradigm	48 Semiotics
36 Phenomenology	49 Significance
37 Positivism	50 Simulation
38 Primary and secondary sources	51 Statistical analysis
39 Probability	52 Systematic review
40 Problem solving	53 Time driven (vs event driven)
41 Problematising	54 Trial and error
42 Proposition	

(www.drannelee.wordpress.com)

References

Abernethy, A. (2006) Rethinking the PhD in English. In C.M. Golde & G.E. Walker (Eds.), *Envisioning the future of doctoral education: Preparing stewards of the discipline*. San Francisco, CA: Jossey-Bass.

Acker, S., Hill, T. & Black, E. (1994) Thesis supervision in the social sciences: Managed or negotiated? *Higher Education*, 28, 483–498.

Ackerlind, G. (2008) A phenomenographic approach to developing academics' understanding of the nature of teaching and learning. *Teaching in Higher Education*, 13(6), 633–644.

Argyris, C. & Schon, D.A. (1974) *Theory in practice: Increasing professional effectiveness*. San Francisco, CA: Jossey-Bass.

Ball, C., Metcalf, J., Pearce, E. & Shinton, S. (2009) *What do PhDs do?* Cambridge: Careers Research and Advisory Centre (CRAC) Ltd.

Bandura, A. (1994) Self-efficacy. *Encyclopaedia of Human Behaviour*, 4, 71–81. www.des.emory.edu/mfp/BanEncy.html (accessed 29.11.09).

Barnett, R. (2000) *Realizing the university in an age of supercomplexity*. Buckingham: SRHE/Open University Press.

Barnett, R. (2004) Learning for an unknown future. *Higher Education Research and Development*, 23(3), 247–260.

Barnett, R. (2009) Knowing and becoming in the higher education curriculum. *Studies in Higher Education*, 34(4), 429–440.

Barnett, R. (2018) *The ecological university: A feasible utopia*. Abingdon: Routledge.

Barrie, S.C. (2004) A research-based approach to generic graduate attributes policy. *Higher Education Research and Development*, 23(3), 261–275.

Barrie, S.C. (2006) Understanding what we mean by the generic attributes of graduates. *Higher Education: The International Journal of Higher Education and Educational Planning*, 51(2), 215–241.

Beaty, L. (2003) *Action learning*. York: Generic Centre.

Becher, T. & Trowler, P. (1989) *Academic tribes and territories*. Buckingham: SHRE/Open University Press.

Becher, T. & Trowler, P. (2001) *Academic tribes and territories* (2nd ed.). Buckingham: SHRE/Open University Press.

Becker, L. & Denicolo, P. (2012) *Publishing journal articles*. London: Sage.

Berglass. S. (2002) The very real dangers of executive coaching. *Harvard Business Review*, 80(6), 86–93.

Biggs, J. & Tang, C. (2007) *Teaching for quality learning at university* (3rd ed.). Buckingham: SRHE/Open University Press.

Biglan, A. (1973a) The characteristics of subject matter in different scientific areas. *Journal of Applied Psychology*, 57(3), 195–203.

Biglan, A. (1973b) The relationships between subject matter characteristics and the structure and output of university departments. *Journal of Applied Psychology*, 57(3), 204–213.

Boote, D. (2006) Learning from the literature. In A. Lee & S. Danby (Eds.) (2012) *Reshaping doctoral education: International approaches and pedagogies*. Abingdon: Routledge.

Boud, D., Keogh, R. & Walker, D. (1985) Promoting reflection in learning: A model. In D. Boud, R. Keogh & D. Walker (Eds.), *Reflection: Turning experience into learning*. London: Kogan Page.

Brennan, J. & Shah, T. (2003) *Report on the implementation of progress files*. London: Centre for Higher Education Research and Information.

Brookfield, S. (1995) *Becoming a critically reflective teacher*. San Francisco, CA: Jossey-Bass.

Browne, M.N. & Freeman, K. (2000) Distinguishing features of critical thinking classrooms. *Teaching in Higher Education*, 5(3), 301–309.

Bryan, B. & Guccione, K. (2018) Was it worth it? A qualitative exploration into graduate perceptions of doctoral value. *Higher Education Research & Development*, 37(6),112–1140. doi: 10.1080/07294360.2018.1479378

Burchfield, R.W. (Ed.) (1996) *Fowler's modern English usage*. Oxford: Clarendon Press.

Burden, P. & Lee, A. (2006) *Personal development planning: A resources guide for academic staff*. Guildford: University of Surrey.

Calderhead, J. & Gates, P. (1993) *Conceptualising reflection in teacher development*. London: Falmer Press.

Carr, W. & Kemmis, S. (1986) *Becoming critical: Education, knowledge, and action research*. Lewes: Falmer Press.

Carson, B.H. (1996) Thirty years of stories: The professor's place in student memories. *Change*, 28(6), 10–17.

Carter, S. & Laurs, D. (Eds.) (2018) *Developing research writing*. Abingdon: Routledge.

Casey, B.H. (2009). The economic contribution of PhDs. *Journal of Higher Education Policy and Management*, 31(3), 219–227.

Clarke, G. & Lunt, I. (2014) The concept of 'originality' in the PhD: How is it interpreted by examiners? *Assessment and Evaluation in Higher Education*, 39 (7), 803–820.

Clarkson, P. (1995) *Change in organisations*. London: Whurr Publishers Ltd.

Clutterbuck, D. & Ragins, B.R. (2002) *Mentoring and diversity*. Oxford: Butterworth Heinemann.

Cotterall, S. (2011) Doctoral students' writing: Where's the pedagogy? *Teaching in Higher Education*, 16(4), 413–425.

Cousin, G. (2009) *Researching learning in higher education*. New York and Abingdon: Routledge.

Cousin, G. & Deepwell, F. (2005) Designs for network learning: A communities of practice perspective. *Studies in Higher Education*, 30(1), 57–66.

Cowan, J. (2008) *On becoming an innovative university teacher: Reflection in action.* Buckingham: SHRE/Open University Press.

Cumming, J. & Kiley, M. (2009) *Research graduate skills project.* Strawberry Hills, NSW: Australian Learning and Teaching Council. www.altc.edu.au/resource-research-skill-development-questions-anu-2009 (accessed 05.12.10).

Darling, L.A. (1985) What do nurses want in a mentor? *Journal of Nursing Administration*, 14(10), 42–44.

Dearing, R. (1997) *Higher education in the learning society.* Norwich: HMSO.

Debowski, S. (2017) *Developing academics: The essential higher education handbook.* London and New York: Routledge.

Dewey, J. (1933) *How we think: A restatement of the relation of reflective thinking to the educative process.* Lexington, MA: D.C. Heath and Company.

Donald, J.G. (2002) *Learning to think.* San Francisco, CA: Jossey-Bass.

Egan, G. (2002) *The skilled helper.* Pacific Grove, CA: Brooks/Cole Thomson Learning.

EHEA. (2018) *The framework of qualifications for the European Higher Education Area.* www.ehea.info/media.ehea.info/file/2018_Paris/77/8/EHEAParis2018_Communique_AppendixIII_952778.pdf (accessed 14. 12.18).

Elkana, Y. (2006) Unmasking uncertainties and embracing contradictions. In C.M. Golde & G.E. Walker (Eds.), *Envisioning the future of doctoral education: Preparing stewards of the discipline.* San Francisco, CA: Jossey-Bass.

Else, H. (2015) How to give the next generation of scholars a career boost. *Times Higher Education Supplement*, 15 January 2015. www.timeshighereducation.com/features/how-to-give-the-next-generation-of-scholars-a-career-boost/2017878.article (accessed 19.11.18).

EUA. (2007) *Doctoral programmes in Europe's universities: Achievements and challenges.* Brussels: European University Association.

EUA. (2010) *Salzburg II – recommendations.* https://eua.eu/resources/publications/615:salzburg-ii-%E2%80%93-recommendations.html (accessed 18. 04.19).

EUA. (2017) *Doctoral education in Europe today: Approaches and institutional structures.* https://eua.eu/downloads/publications/online%20eua%20cde%20survey%2016.01.2019.pdf (accessed 18. 04.19).

Fillery-Travis, A., Maguire, K., Pizzolatti, N., Robinson, L., Lowley, A., Stel, N., Mans, P., van Wijk, J., Prodi, E., Sprerotti, F., Dobrinski, C., Peacock, J., Taylor, R., Vitale, T. & Lee, A. (2017) *Insights from practice: A handbook for supervisors of modern doctorate candidates.* http://superprofdoc.eu/wp-content/uploads/2017/09/SuperProfDoc-handbook-2017.pdf (accessed 03. 10.18).

Freeman, R. (1998) *Mentoring in general practice.* Oxford: Butterworth Heinemann.

Gatfield, T.J. (2005) An investigation into PhD supervisory management styles: Development of a dynamic conceptual model and its managerial implications. *Journal of Higher Education Policy and Management*, 27(3), 311–325.

Golde, C.M. & Walker, G.E. (Eds.) (2006) *Envisioning the future of doctoral education: Preparing stewards of the discipline.* San Francisco, CA: Jossey-Bass.

Grant, B.M. (2005) The pedagogy of graduate supervision: Figuring the relations between supervisor and student. PhD thesis, University of Auckland, Aotearoa.

Grant, B.M. (2008) Agonistic struggle – master–slave dialogues in humanities supervision. *Arts and Humanities in Higher Education*, 7(1), 9–27.

Gregory, J. (2006) Facilitation and facilitator style. In P. Jarvis, *The theory and practice of teaching* (2nd ed.). London: Routledge.

Grenyer, B.F.S. (2002) *Mastering relationship conflicts: Discoveries in theory, research, and practice.* Washington, DC: American Psychological Association.

Guccione, K. (2018) *Trust me! Building and breaking professional trust in doctoral student–supervisor relationships.* London: Leadership Foundation.

Halse. C. & Malfroy, J. (2010) Retheorising doctoral supervision as professional work. *Studies in Higher Education*, 35(1), 79–92.

Hargreaves, J. (2008) Risk: The ethics of a creative curriculum. *Innovations in Education and Teaching International*, 45(3), 227–234.

Harkin, J. (1998) Constructs used by vocational students in England to evaluate their teachers. *Journal of Vocational Education and Training: The Vocational Aspect of Education*, 50(3), 339–353.

Harrison, R. (2002) *Learning and development* (3rd ed.). London: Chartered Institute of Personnel Development.

Hawkins, P. (2006) Coaching supervision. In J. Passmore (Ed.), *Excellence in coaching*. London: Kogan Page.

Haynes, K., Metcalf, J. & Yilmaz, M. (2016) *What do research staff do next?* 'What do researchers do?' series by Vitae. Cambridge: Careers Research and Advisory Centre (CRAC) Ltd.

Hirvela, A. & Yi, Y. (2008) From expectations to empowerment. In C.P. Casanave & X. Li (Eds.), *Learning the literacy practices of graduate school* (pp. 121–133). Ann Arbor, MI: University of Michigan Press.

Hockey, J. (1994) New territory: Problems of adjusting to the first year of a social science PhD. *Studies in Higher Education*, 19(2), 177–190.

Hockey, J. (1996) Contractual solution to problems in the supervision of PhD degrees in the UK. *Studies in Higher Education*, 21(3), 359–371.

Hunt, W., Jagger, N., Metcalfe, J. & Pollard, E. (2010) *What do researchers do? Doctoral graduate destinations and impact three years on.* Cambridge: Careers Research and Advisory Centre (CRAC) Ltd.

Hutchings, W. (2007) *Enquiry-based learning: Definitions and rationale.* Centre for Excellence in Enquiry-Based Learning Essays and Studies, University of Manchester. www.campus.manchester.ac.uk/ceebl/resources/papers/hutchings2007_defi ningebl.pdf (accessed 29.11.09).

Ives, G. & Rowley, G. (2005) Supervisor selection or allocation and continuity of supervision: PhD students' progress and outcomes. *Studies in Higher Education*, 30(5), 535–555.

Jackson, D. & Michelson, G. (2015) Factors influencing the employment of Australian PhD graduates. *Studies in Higher Education*, 40(9), 1600–1679.

Johnson, D.W. & Johnson, R.T. (2001) Co-operation and conflict: Effects on cognition and metacognition. In A. Costa, *Developing minds: A resource book for teaching thinking.* Alexandria, VA: Association for Supervision and Curriculum Development.

Kamler, B. & Thomson, P. (2006) *Helping doctoral students write: Pedagogies for supervision.* London: Routledge.

Kember, D. (2000) Misconceptions about the learning approaches, motivation, and study practices of Asian students. *Higher Education*, 40(1), 99–121.

Kiley, M. (2006) 'Expectation' particularly in a cross-cultural postgraduate research experience. Unpublished paper for supervisor workshops. Canberra: Australian National University.

Kinchin, I.M. & Hay, D.B. (2007) The myth of the research-led teacher. *Teachers and Teaching: Theory and Practice*, 13(1), 43–61.

Kleiman, P. (2008) Towards transformation: Conceptions of creativity in higher education. *Innovations in Education and Teaching International*, 45(3), 209–217.

Kram, K.E. (1985) *Mentoring at work: Developmental relationships in organisational life*. Glenview, IL: Scott, Foresman and Company.

Kulej, G. & Park, C. (2008) PRES 2008 initial results. Higher Education Academy Annual Conference, Harrogate, 1 July.

Kumar, V. & Stracke, E. (2018) Reframing doctoral examination as teaching. *Innovations in Education and Teaching International*, 55(2), 219–227.

Lave, J. & Wenger, E. (1991) *Situated learning: Legitimate peripheral participation*. Cambridge: Cambridge University Press.

Lee, A. (2006) Can you recognise a good facilitator when you see one? *Educational Developments*. London: SEDA. http://epubs.surrey.ac.uk/info_sci/2/(accessed 29. 11.09).

Lee, A. (2007) How can a mentor support experiential learning? *Journal of Clinical Child Psychology and Psychiatry*, 12(3),333–340. http://epubs.surrey.ac.uk/info_sci/4/(accessed 29. 11.09).

Lee, A. (2008) *Supervisory teams: Making them work*. London: Society for Research into Higher Education (SRHE).

Lee, A. (2018a) How can we develop supervisors for the modern doctorate? *Studies in Higher Education*, 43(5), 878–890. doi: 10.1080/03075079.2018.1438116

Lee, A. (2018b) Setting up frameworks: Five approaches to supporting students writing in English as an additional language. In S. Carter & D. Laurs (Eds.), *Developing research writing*. Abingdon and New York: Routledge.

Lee, A. (2019) *Successful research supervision: Advising students doing research*. Abingdon and New York: Routledge.

Murray, R. (2006) *How to write a thesis*. Buckingham: Open University Press.

Murray, R. (2008) (Ed.) *The scholarship of teaching and learning in higher education (helping students to learn)*. Maidenhead: Open University Press/McGraw-Hill.

Murray, R. (2011) *How to write a thesis* (3rd ed.). Maidenhead: Open University Press/McGraw-Hill.

Nygaard, L. (2017) *Writing your master's thesis: From A to zen*. Los Angeles, CA: Sage.

Okorocha, E. (2007) *Supervising international students*. London: Society for Research into Higher Education.

Ottowell, K. (2018) Looking behind the writing: Cultural difficulties facing novice postgraduate second-language (L2) writers in English. *Higher Education in Russia and Beyond*, 2(16), 23–24.

Paltridge, B. & Starfield, S. (2007) *Thesis and dissertation writing in a second language*. Abingdon: Routledge.

Pearson, M. & Brew, A. (2002) Research training and supervision development. *Studies in Higher Education*, 27(2), 135–150.

Perkins, D. (1999) The many faces of constructivism. *Educational Leadership*, 57(3), 6–11.

Perry, W.J. (1970) *Forms of intellectual and ethical development in the college years.* New York: Holt, Rinehart and Winston.

Prins, F.J., de Kleijn, R. & van Tartwijk, J. (2017) Students' use of a rubric for research theses. *Assessment & Evaluation in Higher Education*, 42(1), 128–150.

QAA. (2001) *QAA Guidelines on HE progress files.* www.qaa.ac.uk/academicinfras tructure/progressFiles/guidelines/progfile2001.pdf (accessed 29. 11.09).

QAA. (2008) *QAA benchmark statements.* www.qaa.ac.uk/academicinfrastructure/ FHEQ/EWNI08/default.asp (accessed 29. 11.09).

Quinn Patton, M. (1990) *Qualitative evaluation and research methods.* London and New Delhi: Sage.

Reeves, J., Denicolo, P., Metcalfe, J. & Roberts, J. (2012) *The Vitae researcher development framework and researcher development statement: Methodology and validation report.* Cambridge: Careers Research and Advisory Centre (CRAC) Ltd.

Reymert, I., Nesje, K. & Thune, T. (2017) *A survey of doctoral candidates in Norway.* Oslo: Nordic Institute for Studies in Innovation, Research and Education.

Roach, A., Rieger, E. & Christensen, B.K. (In press) The essential ingredients of research supervision: A discrete-choice experiment. *Journal of Educational Psychology.*

Ryan, Y. & Zuber-Skerritt, O. (1999) *Supervising postgraduates from non-English speaking backgrounds.* Buckingham: SHRE/Open University Press.

Salovey, P. & Mayer, J. (1997) What is emotional intelligence? In P. Salovey & D. Sluyter (Eds.), *Emotional development and emotional intelligence: Implications for educators* (pp. 3–31). New York: Basic Books.

Schon, D. (1991) *The reflective practitioner.* Aldershot: Ashgate.

Shalfawi, S.A.I. (2016) Developing doctoral supervision course assignment (unpub- lished work produced for the University of Stavanger, excerpts reproduced by per- mission from the author).

Slight, C. (2017) *Postgraduate research experience survey 2017: Experiences and personal outlook of postgraduate researchers.* York: Higher Education Academy. www.heacademy.ac.uk/knowledge-hub/postgraduate-research-experience-survey- report-2017 (accessed 18.04.19).

Smith, B. (1997) *Lecturing to large groups.* Birmingham: Staff & Educational Devel- opment Association.

Spencer Oatey, H. & Stadler, S. (2009) *The global people competency framework – com- petencies for effective intercultural interaction.* Warwick: Centre for Applied Linguis- tics, University of Warwick. www.globalpeople.org.uk/ (accessed 29.11.09).

Sternberg, R.J. & Lubart, T. (1995) *Defying the crowd: Cultivating creativity in a culture of conformity.* New York: The Free Press.

Stevenson, P. & Brand, A. (2006) Exploring the developmental impacts of complet- ing a postgraduate certificate in learning and teaching. *Educational Developments*, 7 (3). London: SEDA.

Strunk, W. Jr. & White, E.B. (2011) *The elements of style.* www.gutenberg.org/files/ 37134/37134-h/37134-h.htm (accessed 17. 04.19).

Swales, J.M. & Feak, C.B. (2004) *Academic writing for graduate students* (2nd ed.). Ann Arbor, MI: University of Michigan Press.

Swartz, R. & Perkins, D.N. (1990) *Teaching thinking: Issues and approaches*. Pacific Grove, CA: Midwest Publications.

Taylor, E.W. (2007) An update of transformative learning theory: A critical review of the empirical research (1999–2005). *International Journal of Lifelong Education*, 26(2), 173–191.

Taylor, M. (1979) *Coverdale on management*. London: Heinemann.

Taylor, S., Kiley, M. & Humphrey, R. (2018) *A handbook for doctoral supervisors* (2nd ed.). Abingdon: Routledge.

Thomson, J.A.K. (2004) *Nicomachean ethics* (revised by H. Tredennick). London: Penguin.

Thune, T., Kyvik, S.S., Olsen, T.B., Vabo, A. & Tomte, C. (2012) *PhD education in a knowledge society*. Oslo: Nordic Institute for Studies in Innovation, Research and Education.

Tosey, P. & McDonnell, J. (2006) *Mapping enquiry-based learning: Discourse, fractals and a bowl of cherries*. L2L Working Paper. www.som.surrey.ac.uk/learningto learn/documents/mappingEBL.pdf (accessed 29. 11.09).

Trafford, V. & Leshem, S. (2008) *Stepping stones to achieving your doctorate: By focussing on your viva from the start*. Maidenhead: McGraw-Hill/Open University Press.

Vailes, F. (2017) *The flourishing student*. Bramley, UK: Practical Inspiration Publishing.

Vardy, P. & Grosch, P. (1999) *The puzzle of ethics*. London: Fount.

Vitae. (2008) *The Concordat to support the career development of researchers*. www .bristol.ac.uk/media-library/sites/staffdevelopment/documents/rs-hub/Vitae-Concordat-Vitae-2011.pdf (accessed 19. 11.18).

Walsh, E., Hargreaves, C., Hillemann-Delaney, U. & Li, J. (2015) Doctoral researchers' views on entrepreneurship: Ranging from 'a responsibility to improve the future' to 'a dirty word'. *Studies in Higher Education*, 40(5), 775–790. doi: 10.1080/03075079.2013.842219

Weinstein, K. (1999) *Action learning – a practical guide*. Aldershot: Gower.

Wellington, J. (2013) Searching for 'doctorateness'. *Studies in Higher Education*, 38 (10), 1490–1503.

Wisker, G. (2012) *The good supervisor* (2nd ed.). Basingstoke: Palgrave Macmillan.

Wisker, G., Robinson, G., Trafford, V., Creighton, E. & Warnes, M. (2003a) Recognising and overcoming dissonance in postgraduate student research. *Studies in Higher Education*, 28(1), 91–105.

Wisker, G., Robinson, G., Trafford, V., Lilly, J. & Warnes, M. (2003b) Supporting postgraduate student learning through supervisory practices. In C. Rust (Ed.), *Improving student learning: Theory research and scholarship*. Oxford: OCSLD.

Further reading/other sources consulted

Becker, J., Niehaves, B. & Klose, K. (2005) A framework for epistemological perspectives on simulation. *Journal of Artificial Societies and Social Simulation*, 8 (4). http://jasss.soc.surrey.ac.uk/8/4/1.html

Bitchener, J., Basturkmen, H., East, M. & Meyer, H. (2011) Best practice in supervisor feedback on student thesis writing. http://akoaotearoa.ac.nz/download/

ng/file/group-1659/best-practice-in-supervisor-feedback-to-thesis-students.pdf (accessed 17.04.19).

Costa, A. (Ed.) (2001) *Developing minds: A resource book for teaching thinking.* Alexandria, VA: Association for Supervision and Curriculum Development.

Cottrell, A. (2011) *Critical thinking skills.* Basingstoke: Palgrave Macmillan.

Epstein, R.L. (2006) *Critical thinking.* Belmont, CA: Thomson Wadsworth.

Fung, D. (2017) *A connected curriculum.* London: UCL Press. www.ucl.ac.uk/ucl-press/browse-books/a-connected-curriculum-for-higher-education (accessed 03.10.18).

Grant, B. (2015) The hauntings of doctoral supervision in post-colonial contexts. Society for Research into Higher Education seminar, London, 16 September.

Hofstede, G., Hofstede, G.J. & Minkov, M. (2010) *Cultures and organisations: Software of the mind.* New York: McGraw Hill.

Jackson, C. & Tinkler, P. (2007) *A guide for internal and external doctoral examiners.* London: Society for Research into Higher Education.

Lee, A. (2007) Personal development planning and the economics tribe. *International Review of Economics Education*, 6(1), 27–47.

Lee, A. (2008a) How are doctoral students supervised? Concepts of research supervision. *Studies in Higher Education*, 33(4), 267–281.

Lee, A. (2008b) Teaching master's programmes and doctoral supervision: At the boundary of research and teaching. Conference Proceedings for Scholarship of Teaching and Learning Conference, London.

Lee, A. (2009a) Some implications of European initiatives for doctoral supervision. In E. Froment, J. Kohler, L. Purser & L. Wilson (Eds.), *EUA Bologna handbook: Making Bologna work.* Berlin: Raabe Verlag.

Lee, A. (2009b) The postdoctoral researcher – aiming high. An initial survey of the literature. Commissioned review for Vitae UK (CRAC).

Lee, A. (2010a) Developments in postgraduate education and their implications for research supervision. In J. Murphy, C. Griffin & B. Higgs (Eds.), *Research–Teaching Linkages: Practice & Policy.* Cork: National Academy for the Integration of Research and Teaching and Learning (NAIRTL).

Lee, A. (2010b) New approaches to doctoral supervision: Implications for educational developers. *Educational Developments*, 11 (2). London: SEDA.

Lee A. (2012a) *Successful research supervision: Advising students doing research.* London and New York: Routledge.

Lee, A. (2012b) *The future of post-graduate education – a briefing document.* London: Westminster Higher Education Forum.

Lee, A. (2013a) Are our doctoral programmes doing what we think they are? *Journal of Public Policy and Management*, 33(2).

Lee, A. (2013b) What makes a really good support programme for part-time lecturers in higher education? In F. Beaton & A. Gilbert (Eds.), *Developing effective part-time teachers in HE.* London and New York: Routledge.

Lee, A. (2014a) New approaches to CPD and preparing academics for supervision. In D. Halliday (Ed.), *International Conference on Developments in Doctoral Education and Training. Conference Proceedings.* Lichfield: UKCGE.

Lee, A. (2014b) Generic support for doctoral researchers in the UK. In S. Carter & D. Laurs (Eds.), *Developing generic support for doctoral students.* Abingdon: Routledge.

Lee, A. (2014c) Professional skills development. In S. Carter & D. Laurs (Eds.), *Developing generic support for doctoral students.* Abingdon: Routledge.

Lee, A. & Green, B. (2009) Supervision as metaphor. *Studies in Higher Education,* 34(6), 615–630.

Lee, A. & Murray, R. (2015) Supervising writing: Helping postgraduate students develop as researchers. *Innovations in Education and Teaching International,* 52 (5), 558–570.

Lee, A. & Pettigrove, M. (2010) *Preparing to teach in higher education.* Lichfield: UKCGE.

Lee, A., Pitt, J., Lee, A. & Griffiths, B. (2010) Higher education without academics? *Educational Developments,* 11 (2). London: SEDA.

Murray, R. & Moore, S. (2006) *The handbook of academic writing.* Maidenhead: Open University Press/McGraw Hill.

Pan, L. & Katrenko, S. (2015) A review of the UK's interdisciplinary research using a citation-based approach. Report to the UK HE funding bodies and MRC by Elsevier. HEFCE (Higher Education Funding Council for England). https://webarchive.nationalarchives.gov.uk/20170712122715/http://www.hefce.ac.uk/pubs/rereports/Year/2015/interdisc/(accessed 17.04.19).

Sword, H. (2012) *Stylish academic writing.* Boston, MA: Harvard University Press.

Tinkler, P. & Jackson, C. (2004) *The doctoral examination process: A handbook for student, examiners and supervisors.* Maidenhead: SRHE/Open University Press.

Tittle, P. (2011) *Critical thinking: An appeal to reason.* New York and London: Routledge

Index

Taylor & Francis eBooks

www.taylorfrancis.com

A single destination for eBooks from Taylor & Francis
with increased functionality and an improved user
experience to meet the needs of our customers.

90,000+ eBooks of award-winning academic content in
Humanities, Social Science, Science, Technology, Engineering,
and Medical written by a global network of editors and authors.

TAYLOR & FRANCIS EBOOKS OFFERS:

A streamlined
experience for
our library
customers

A single point
of discovery
for all of our
eBook content

Improved
search and
discovery of
content at both
book and
chapter level

REQUEST A FREE TRIAL
support@taylorfrancis.com

 Routledge
Taylor & Francis Group

 CRC Press
Taylor & Francis Group